SELF-W
MENTAL MAGIC

67 FOOLPROOF
MIND-READING
TRICKS

KARL FULVES

With 73 Illustrations by JOSEPH K. SCHMIDT

Dover Publications, Inc.
New York

Copyright © 1979 by Karl Fulves.
All rights reserved under Pan American and
International Copyright Conventions.

Self-Working Mental Magic: 67 Foolproof Mind-Reading Tricks is a new work, first published by Dover Publications, Inc., in 1979.

International Standard Book Number: 0-486-23806-7
Library of Congress Catalog Card Number: 79-50010

Manufactured in the United States of America
Dover Publications, Inc.
31 East 2nd Street, Mineola, N.Y. 11501

INTRODUCTION

Magic is the only subject that has been accepted throughout history by all cultures and all levels of society in every part of the world. Magic and the supernatural combine to produce mental magic, telepathy and clairvoyance, the ability to see the future and read minds. Mental magic is the subject of this book.

All of the mental mysteries in this book are accomplished by trickery, but the mentalist has an advantage that the magician does not. When a magician performs tricks with cards, coins, rope or silks, his audience will almost always suspect that there is some secret which explains the trick away. The mentalist is greeted in a strikingly different way. His experiments in extrasensory perception are accepted as real magic. The audience wants to believe that the mentalist has paranormal powers.

The mental routines in this book were chosen with two criteria in mind. The first is that the routines, although self-working, would be strong enough to amaze the average spectator. The second criterion has to do with human nature. Most of the tricks were chosen specifically to involve the spectator on a personal level. In performing many of these routines you will find that the spectator wants you to succeed and will volunteer information that you never asked for. Thus, as you perform these tricks and acquire experience with your audiences, you will learn a great deal about human nature, and that is the key to success in this field.

Mental magic is serious stuff but it need not be dull and boring. In this book a trick like "Katch Koin" (page 33) has an amusing quality, "Fire Power" (page 36) is surprising as well as baffling, and "Super Psychometry" (page 114) is flexible enough to allow for humor even as it bewilders the audience. For your program choose tricks which permit a change of pace and your audience will be both mystified and entertained.

Special thanks to the contributors, and to artist-magician Joseph K. Schmidt, whose illustrations make the tricks easy to understand.

KARL FULVES

CONTENTS

INSTANT ESP

The best way to achieve a reputation as a mind reader is to be able to perform mental tricks on the spur of the moment, without special apparatus. The tricks in this chapter are designed to accomplish this purpose. Using simple props such as matches, coins and cards, you are able to give the impression of great mental powers.

All mental tricks depend on presentation. The methods are usually simple and well concealed. For a mental trick to succeed, you must present it in such a way that your audience is convinced you have extranormal powers.

The tricks in this chapter are selected to give you practice in presentation. The final trick in the chapter is typical of the best mental magic; it depends *entirely* on presentation. The secret lies in what you say, and because of this, the effect you achieve is staggering.

1. MONEY SENSE

Ask a friend to take a penny behind his back, place it in either hand, close each hand into a fist and then bring both hands forward.

Instruct him to spread his arms apart slowly and concentrate on which hand holds the penny. Without hesitation you tell him which hand does indeed contain the penny!

METHOD: This quick trick will work most of the time. As in most mental magic, even if it fails you will get credit for attempting a difficult feat of mind reading. The secret, as described by Stuart Robson, is a curious one. You do not look at the spectator's hands to find out which hand contains the coin. You look at his nose.

For some reason, as the spectator moves his hands apart from one another, his nose will usually point in the direction of the hand containing the penny. You must do this trick without really stopping to analyze any slight tilt of the spectator's head. Strive to obtain an instant impression.

This is the basic trick as it might be performed by a magician. If you want to add an element of exotic mystery, use an old coin or amulet instead of a penny. Hand the amulet to a spectator and tell him that it's left-handed—it knows when it is in someone's left hand and will send out strong mental vibrations. If it is in the right hand it tends to keep quiet. Then follow the procedure mentioned above. With this approach, the spectator's attention is focused on the coin or amulet. If he suspects anything, he suspects the coin of being gimmicked. But this misdirects attention away from the true method and thus strengthens the mystery.

2. SIXTH SENSE

If you are asked to repeat a trick like "Money Sense," it is always wise to use a different method to accomplish the same mystery. The following trick is similar in effect but completely different in method.

In this trick the spectator takes a penny behind his back and places it in either hand. He then brings both hands forward. At the same time you place a penny behind your back and put it in either hand.

The spectator reveals the hand that holds the penny; you reveal that your penny is held in the same hand.

METHOD: The secret is that you use two pennies but the spectator is aware of only one. At the beginning of the trick remove a penny from your pocket and hand it to the spectator. Instruct him to put it behind his back and secretly place it in either his left hand or his right hand.

You then reach into your pocket and say that you will try to guess which hand he chooses. To do this you will use another penny. In fact you remove two pennies from the pocket. Don't show them. Place them behind your back.

Say to the spectator, "I'm going to try to guess which hand you'll choose. I'll use this coin to indicate my guess." With both hands behind your back, place one penny in your left hand and one in your right.

Close both hands into fists and bring them out into view. Ask the spectator to bring his closed fists into view. Ask him to reveal which hand contains his penny. If he shows it is his left hand, open your left hand to show that you placed the penny in the same hand.

You may repeat the trick once more, but do not do it more than that because the spectator may guess that you are using two pennies. Objects other than coins may be used—paper clips or any small objects that fit easily in the hand, providing you have easy access to a pair for you to use.

3. THE BLINDFOLDED DECK

If a deck of cards is handy you are always able to perform this amazing feat of prophecy. The method was kept in complete secrecy for years and was used to fool magicians as well as laymen.

When a borrowed, well-shuffled deck is handed to you, remark that you will shortly have a spectator cut the deck and select a card. State that you will try to predict exactly where he will cut the deck.

Hold up the deck so that the faces of the cards are toward you, and look through it as if to decide where the spectator will cut. Actually, you look at and remember the *top card* of the deck.

Close the deck and place it face-down on the table. Then pick up a sheet of paper, write the name of the top card, fold the paper and place it under a drinking glass or teacup. Do not let the spectator see your prediction.

Now say, "To make this really difficult, we'll blindfold the deck." Put the deck face-down on your left hand and drape an opaque pocket handkerchief over the deck. This seems to be what you do, but under the cover of the handkerchief, secretly put your thumb under the deck and lever it over so it is face-up, as shown in Figure 1. The handkerchief completely covers the secret turnover of the deck.

Rest the deck on the upturned palm of your left hand, under the handkerchief. Now ask a spectator to cut off a portion of the

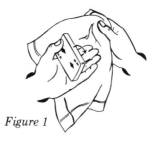

Figure 1

deck. He does this by grasping the sides of the deck through the handkerchief and lifting up a packet of cards away from the deck.

You will now apparently take the bottom part of the deck out from under the handkerchief so he can see the card he cut to. But as your left hand, holding its packet of cards, moves down and away from the packet held by the spectator, your left fingers curl in, causing the packet to pivot over to a face-down condition, Figure 2. (The handkerchief is indicated by a dotted line.)

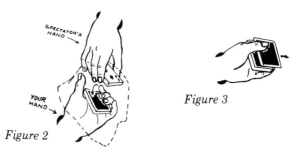

Figure 3

Figure 2

Now bring this packet out from under the handkerchief and have the spectator remove the top card of the packet, Figure 3. It appears as if this is the card he cut to, but because of the subtle handling, it is really the card that was originally on top of the deck.

When the spectator has taken the card, put your left hand back up under the handkerchief to return the packet to the rest of the deck. As you do, secretly flip the packet over with the thumb so that it is face-up again. This action is the same as that depicted in Figure 1.

Have the spectator release the packet he cut. Then, using your right hand, lift up the entire deck through the handkerchief. Using both hands, wrap the deck up in the hand-kerchief and place it on the table.

Ask the spectator for the name of his card. Then have him open the slip of papers. He will be amazed that you were able to know beforehand which card he chose.

4. THE FIGURES MATCH

A spectator chooses a three-digit number at random. You then tell him what the three digits are. No questions are asked. This is a good trick to do as an after-dinner demonstration because it is impromptu and works best when done while seated at a table.

You will need a sheet of paper and a pencil with which the spectator can jot down the numbers. But the key to the trick is a new book of matches. Most people do not know that a new book of matches contains exactly 20 matches. This is the key to the success of this demonstration.

METHOD: When you want to perform "The Figures Match," take a new matchbook and remove and discard two matches, leaving 18. Then arrange to have the matchbook on the table in plain sight.

Ask a spectator to jot down a three-digit number while your back is turned. To make the trick more personalized, request that he choose a number that has some meaning to him. He can decide on three digits of his Social-Security number, three digits of his license plate number, etc. To make the test more interesting, tell him that each digit should be between 1 and 9, and that each digit should be different.

Say the number he chooses is 238. Ask him to think of the number backwards to form a new number. In our example he would reverse the digits and get the number 832.

Ask him to subtract the smaller number from the larger number. Remember that he does this while your back is turned. After he has performed the subtraction, he will get, in our example, 594.

Have the spectator note the smallest digit in his result. Then tell him to remove that many matches from the book. From our example, he would note that the smallest digit in 594 is 4, so he would remove 4 matches from the book.

Tell him to place the matches he just removed on the paper, fold the paper and place it in his pocket. Finally, have him hand you the matchbook behind you back.

When you get the matchbook, remove matches one at a time and drop them into view on the table. Continue doing this until you have dropped exactly 9 matches on the table. Do not call attention to the number of matches. Merely toss them out onto the table.

After the 9 matches have been disposed of, take the matchbook from behind your back and note the number of matches it contains. In our example, it will contain 5 matches. Mentally subtract 5 from 9 and you know that the spectator has exactly 4 matches in his pocket.

Further, you know that of the three digits the spectator wrote, not only is the smallest digit 4, but the next smallest digit is 5, exactly corresponding to the number of matches left in the book. This result always holds true, no matter which three-digit number the spectator started with.

Remark that there is a correlation between numbers and a person's character. This correlation is part of the larger study of numerology. Then go on to reveal that the number of matches the spectator has in his pocket, wrapped up in paper, is exactly 4. Remove the 5 matches from the packet and hand them to the spectator as you say, "I see another digit in the number you chose. Your personality is of the 4-5 type, so I'd guess the other digit is a 5."

5. SQUARING THE CYCLE

On a sheet of paper draw the layout illustrated in Figure 4. The only other prop you will need is an ordinary die. The size of

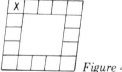

Figure 4

the squares in the layout should be the same as the dimensions of one side of the die.

When you have finished drawing the layout, turn your back. Have the spectator choose a number on the die and place it on the crossed square with the chosen number facing down.

Now ask him to move the die along the layout one square at a time. As he does this, he is to give the die a quarter-turn forward each time he advances to a new square on the layout.

He can move the die any number of squares he desires as long as he gives the die a quarter-turn each time he advances to a new square. When he is satisfied that the die is on a random square, he tells you and you turn around.

You do not know the number he started with and you ask no questions. You do not touch the die at first, but you merely concentrate on it. Then you move the die from square to square, turning it a quarter-turn as you move to each square. Finally you stop. The number now showing on top of the die is the very number originally chosen by the spectator!

METHOD: After the spectator has noted a number and moved the die around to a random spot on the layout, turn around and pretend to concentrate. Say that you will try to receive a mental impression from the die. To pantomime doing this, place your palm-down right hand above the die and slowly rotate the hand in a circular motion.

Act satisfied. Then move the die from square to square, one square at a time, giving it a quarter-turn each time, until you reach one of the crossed squares shown in Figure 5. (These

 Figure 5

squares have crosses on them in this diagram only for your reference. In actual performance there is only one cross on the layout, at the position shown in Figure 4. The crosses indicated in Figure 5 will have to be committed to memory, but that isn't difficult; they fall in the exact middle of each side.)

When you have moved the die back to any one of the crossed squares shown in Figure 5 (always remembering to give the die a quarter-turn as you move it from square to square), the die will end up with the chosen number uppermost.

6. SIGNIFICANT DIGIT

A sheet of paper is folded in half. A circle is placed at the center of each half. While you turn your back, a spectator fills in one of the circles with his lucky number. He then places the paper writing-side down on the table.

Turn around and tear the paper in half along the fold. There are now two pieces of paper. One of them contains the spectator's number. Without asking a question, you are able to tell the spectator which piece of paper contains the number. Then, without hesitation, and without asking a single question, you name the exact number!

METHOD: This trick is an ideal follow-up to "The Figures Match" (page 5) because a similar effect is brought about by completely different means. Use a piece of paper or index card measuring about 3 inches by 5 inches. Fold it in half. Then put a circle in the center of each half. The circles should each be about the size of a dime.

Turn your back. Have a spectator think of a number from 1 to 9. Again try to personalize his choice by asking him if he has a lucky number. If he does, instruct him to use that number.

While you turn your back he writes the number in either circle on the card (but not in both circles). When he has done this, have him put the paper on the table with the writing side down.

While your back is turned, secretly place the right forefinger against your lips and transfer a bit of moisture to it. Then put the hands together and transfer some of the saliva to the left forefinger. If you have naturally moist hands, this procedure is not necessary.

After the spectator has completed the writing, take the paper between your hands and tear it in half along the fold, as shown in Figure 6. This is where the secret comes into play.

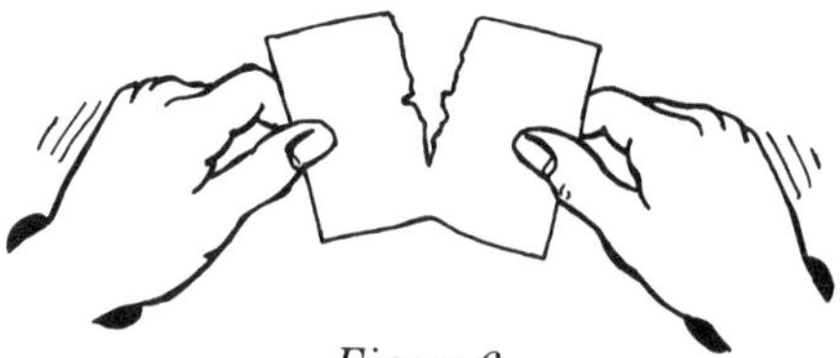

Figure 6

Note that the first finger of each hand rests naturally against the writing side of the paper when you tear the paper in half. Each finger actually rests against the penciled circle on each part of the paper. Hold the paper firmly as you tear it, so that you will pick up an impression of the writing on the forefinger of one hand.

After tearing the paper, place the pieces on the table face down. Secretly note whether the impression of the writing is on the right or left forefinger and you know which piece of paper contains the spectator's writing. A glance at the forefinger will also tell you the digit the spectator wrote.

Build up the ending of the trick. Pretend to have great difficulty getting a mental impression of which piece of paper has the spectator's writing. Then reveal the correct piece of paper. When the spectator verifies that you are right, have him cover that piece of paper with his hand.

Again concentrate, back away from the table, stall for dramatic effect, and finally reveal the number. Although the means is simple, the end effect is exceptionally strong.

7. MIND POWER

Four ordinary objects are placed on the table. You jot the name of one of them on a slip of paper and place it aside. A spectator then chooses one of the objects. Although the choice is a random one, you have correctly predicted which object would be chosen.

METHOD: The four objects are a glass, a cup, a saltshaker and a matchbook. All are usually available at the dinner table or in a restaurant. There is no preparation. Simply group the four objects in a row on the table. What follows is a swindle, but an impressive one.

On a sheet of paper write, "You will pick the glass." Fold the slip and have the spectator hold it in his left hand. Tell him to close his eyes and hold his right hand palm-down over the four objects.

When he has closed his eyes, arrange the four objects as shown in Figure 7, with the glass in the middle. Direct the spectator to lower his hand slowly, still keeping his eyes closed, until his hand touches one of the four objects.

Figure 7

The swindle is this. Because the glass is the tallest object, his hand will touch the glass first. If so, have the prediction opened and verified.

If you're working with the spectator alone and there is no one else around, there is a way to make the prediction ironclad. Have him close his eyes and slowly lower his hand until he touches an object. As he lowers his hand, quietly maneuver the glass to a position under his hand. His hand must then contact the glass with no chance of failure.

8. HYPNO-MATH

The Devil is notorious for tricking the unwary into losing wagers. Almost always the wager is a simple one, and almost always the Devil wins the bet. The mentalist offers to demonstrate just such a devilish wager using two numbers which the Devil claims exert a strange power over people.

These numbers are so elusive they can't be added together correctly, no matter how good a person is at arithmetic. To illustrate, the mentalist jots down two sets of numbers. One set can be added easily but the other seems to create a hypnotic spell and refuses to be added.

A spectator tries his hand at adding each set of numbers. His arithmetic is checked by another spectator. It turns out that the first set of numbers was added correctly, but the second set was not.

The curious thing is that no matter how carefully the spectator adds the numbers, he cannot add the second set of numbers correctly.

METHOD: The origin of this routine is unknown but the following version was suggested by Sam Schwartz. On a slip of paper jot down the two sets of numbers shown in Figure 8. You will use this piece of paper, a pencil, and a separate piece of paper to record the spectators' sums.

Hand the first paper to the spectator. Tell him to find the sum of each set of numbers. He is to write his sums on the separate sheet of paper. The sum he gets from the lefthand set will be 797, and the sum from the right 1070. Instruct him not

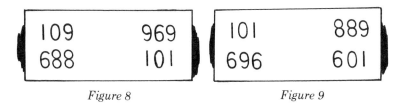

Figure 8   Figure 9

to add aloud, lest he affect the addition of the other spectator.

Take both sheets of paper to another spectator to have the addition checked. As you do this, secretly turn around the piece of paper with the two sets of numbers. The result is shown in Figure 9.

The second spectator checks the sums. He will find that the sum of 797 is correct, but the second sum is not. The spectator wrote down 1070, and the answer should have been 1490.

9. TELE-POKER

Some of the best mind-reading demonstrations are those done over the telephone. They will be long remembered by spectators because of the obvious impossibility of the mentalist knowing anything or his being able to control the spectator's actions. It pays to learn several such tricks so that you are always ready to spring an impossible trick on the person you call. A number of telephone tricks appear in this book. One of the best is this routine.

Calling a friend, the mentalist tells him of a new poker game that can be played long distance. The mentalist asks his friend to bring a deck of cards to the phone.

When the spectator returns to the phone with the deck, tell him you are going to play a card game called "Long-distance Poker." The spectator is told to begin by dealing out two hands. He can decide on any number of cards, but each hand must contain the same number of cards. The mentalist does not know how many cards have been dealt into each hand.

Once the hands are dealt, the mentalist says that the first hand will be his and the second hand the spectator's. To open the game, the mentalist discards one card from his hand by directing the spectator to discard a single card from the mentalist's hand.

Now the mentalist asks, "You must also discard some cards from your hand. It can be any number. How many cards would you like to discard?" The spectator might say three. He therefore discards three cards from his hand.

Then the mentalist says, "Now discard as many cards from my hand as remain in your hand. In other words, if your hand has six cards left, discard six cards from my hand."

After this is done the mentalist brings the game to its surprising conclusion. "I didn't tell you the object of the game at the beginning because it might have influenced your choice. The object is to discard a number of cards from the hands until one player has only two cards left. That player is the winner. I believe that my hand now contains exactly two cards, so I won. You can pay me by mail."

The mentalist's hand *does* contain only two cards, and he hangs up before the stunned spectator can say another word.

METHOD: The trick works itself. Just follow the directions and you will always be the winner. The key to it is in the one question you ask the spectator. When you ask him how many cards he would like to discard, wait for his answer. You then mentally subtract 1 from his answer. The resultant number tells you how many cards are left in your hand. In our example the spectator called out the number 3. Subtract 1 and you have a result of 2. This tells you that your hand will be left with two cards.

If the spectator called out 5, then you would bring the trick to a successful conclusion by saying, "The object of the game is to discard a number of cards from the hands until one player has only *four* cards left." If the spectator did indeed discard five cards, he would find at the finish of the game that the mentalist's hand did contain exactly four cards. Thus, you alter the wording of your concluding statement so that the winning player is the one with one card less that the number called out by the spectator. You are always the winner.

This routine is the author's presentation of a trick of Jack Miller's. The Miller trick is in turn based on a concept that lies behind "Things Equal" later in this book. It will instruct the reader to study how a single concept can produce two such seemingly disparate tricks.

10. A MIND FOR FIGURES

At times the mentalist is willing to take a chance on a trick that does not have a guaranteed outcome. He can afford the risk because, unlike the magician, the mentalist attempts to tap supernormal powers that may not always respond to his wishes.

This routine is of that kind. If you have practiced and performed the preceding tricks, you will find this routine a rewarding challenge. It is a novelty in that there is no method or secret to it. It will work most of the time, and when it does, the result appears incredible. Even if the test does not work completely, it is structured in such a way that it will seem as if the spectator and not the mentalist is having an off day.

It is *all* a matter of presentation, so we will proceed directly with the way the trick is handled. Because the wording is important, you must learn the trick exactly as it is written here. Each sentence is strategically placed to influence the spectator on a subconscious level.

Use two slates or large squares of poster board for maximum visibility. Also try to use chalk of a color that contrasts strongly with the color of the writing surface. If the slate is black or green, use yellow chalk. If the poster board is white, use a black marker or charcoal pencil.

On one slate write the number 37. On the other slate write 68. Make sure the writing is large and clear. You want the numbers as bold as possible for maximum impact when they are later revealed.

Both slates are placed on the table, writing side down. The audience does not know what is written on either slate.

This is the presentation. Facing a spectator you say:

"I'm going to think of a number and I'll try to transmit it to you. Make your mind a blank. Try to clear it of thought patterns. You are going to think of a number.

"The number that I'm thinking of is an odd number. It has

two digits, and they are different from one another. In other words, I'm not thinking of 33, 44, 55, or any number where the digits repeat.

"Are you ready? Remember, my number has two digits and it is an odd number. It's between . . . "

Here you pause. Until this point the spectator was under the impression that you might have been thinking of any two-digit odd number. Now, for the first time he realizes that there is going to be a limit placed on the number. His mind will go blank at this point, and this is exactly what you want.

"The number is between . . . between . . . 10 and 50. Would you please name the first number that comes into your head?"

In most cases the spectator will say 37, or an odd number close to it. Whatever number he names aloud, do not give anything away by the expression on your face. On the slate that has the number 37 written on the bottom surface, write the spectator's number on the top blank surface.

The test now continues:

"Let us try a second number. Again make your mind a blank. I have an even number in mind. It has two digits and both digits are different. Try to guess the number. Remember that it is an even number.

"Are you ready? Good. My number is an even number, it has two digits, and it is between . . . "

Again pause. Then continue, " . . . between 50 and 100. Name the first number that comes into your mind."

In most cases the spectator will think of 68. Whatever the number, write it on the top blank surface of the second slate (the slate that has 68 written on the bottom surface).

The revelation now depends one how accurate the spectator's guesses were. If you do this with a roomful of people, there will be several people in the room who will exclaim, usually with great surprise, that they were in fact thinking of 37 and 68 when they see the numbers you wrote. Thus, even if the spectator you are working with happens to get one or both numbers wrong, you will find that his numbers were close to yours, or that others in the room thought of the same numbers you have on the slates.

Considering that there are dozens of different possibilities, the odds seem high against success. But if you follow the presentation given above, in most cases the spectator will name 37 and 68. The presentation given here is patterned along the lines of Slydini's presentation. It is an outstanding mental feat and well worth the time spent mastering the details.

MIND READING WITH CARDS

Playing cards are always available and they are a convenient means with which to demonstrate mind-reading tests. Strive to make the demonstrations serious. Act as if you are uncertain of the outcome. If you play your part well, the audience will accept each of these routines as examples of psychic powers at work.

All of the tricks described here have ordinary playing cards as the major items of apparatus, but magical depots stock special decks that are used by mentalists. These are ESP decks and Tarot decks. Either ESP or Tarot cards can be used for most of the tricks in this chapter. They are not necessary, but, if used, they tend to add to the general aura of the supernatural.

11. SCRAMBLED THOUGHTS

From a deck of cards you remove the Ace, Two and Three of Clubs. A spectator turns these three cards face-down and mixes them up on the table. Now each of three people takes one card.

Turn your back. Ask two of the three people to exchange cards. Thus, for example, spectator "A" gives his card to "C" and likewise, "C" gives his card to "A."

Now each spectator calls out the name of the card he holds. As soon as the cards are called out, with your back still turned, you are able to tell which two people exchanged cards.

The trick may be repeated. You ask no questions, yet you are able to tell each time which two spectators exchanged cards.

METHOD: Before performing the trick, remove the Ace of Clubs from the deck. Place a small pencil dot at the upper left and lower right corners. Then put the Ace back into the deck. You have marked the Ace in a way that allows you to identify it later on. It is on the basis of this one small piece of information that you are able to tell later which two spectators exchanged cards. The principle was developed by Jack Vosburgh.

When ready to perform the trick, have someone shuffle the deck. Then tell him to remove the Ace, Two and Three of Clubs. When these three cards have been removed, the balance of the deck is placed aside.

The Ace, Two and Three are mixed face-down by the spectator. Ask another spectator to pick any one of the three cards. Another spectator chooses a card, and the third spectator gets the remaining card. Your only task is to remember which spectator gets the marked Ace. We'll call this spectator "A."

Turn your back. Request two of the spectators to secretly exchange cards. Tell them to do so silently so that you don't have a clue as to which two people are involved in the exchange.

With your back still turned, ask each person to tell you the name of the card he now holds. If spectator "A" still holds the Ace, then you know the other two spectators exchanged cards.

If "A" does not still hold the Ace, you know he exchanged cards with the spectator who *now* hold the Ace. Thus, by a simple means you know which two spectators were involved in the exchange. In presenting the trick, remark that you will try to read the minds of two people at once. After the exchange of playing cards, explain that you want the spectator who didn't exchange cards to make his mind a blank. You then go on to reveal which two spectators made the exchange.

12. THE PSYCHIC PICKPOCKET

If a pickpocket were also a psychic, he'd be able to glance at a stranger and know immediately which of the stranger's pockets contained a valuable item. This is the theme of the trick.

While you are out of the room, someone removes the Ace of Spades from the deck and places it in one of his pockets. When this has been done, you are told you can reenter the room.

When you return to the room you explain that, as a psychic, you would make an expert pickpocket because you can tell at glance which pocket has the item you want. Closing your eyes, pat your own pockets, and say, "I think I'd hide the Ace in this pocket if I were you."

When you say this you indicate the left front trouser pocket. The spectator is usually dumbfounded to discover that you chose exactly the pocket that he hid the Ace in.

METHOD: The trick works well in a living room setting. Don't try to perform it all the time, but when circumstances are right you can bring about a seeming miracle.

What it comes down to is not a secret code with someone in the audience (the usual guess spectators make) but something much easier. When you are out of the room and have closed the door behind you, simply peer through the keyhole back into the room you just left!

Before doing this trick, it is wise to go into the adjoining room and check that the keyhole allows you an unobstructed view of events in the living room. If it checks out, then later in the evening you can perform this mysterious feat.

13. DIGIT DISCOVERY

Sometimes a number chosen by a spectator can be revealed in a manner that is especially surprising and baffling. This test starts off in a simple way, but when it is repeated, it is found that the mentalist knew what number a spectator would think of before it was chosen.

The spectator is given a packet of cards. He is asked to think of a number from 1 to 10. While the mentalist turns his back, the spectator transfers a number of cards from the top of the packet to the bottom. The number of cards he transfers is to be equal to the thought-of number. If, for instance, he thought of the number 4, he would transfer 4 cards, one at a time, from top to bottom.

Although the spectator does this silently, when the mentalist turns around and takes the packet, he is able to tell the spectator the thought-of number.

Now the trick is repeated. But first the mentalist places the packet behind his back. He tells the spectator he is going to try to guess the thought-of number before the spectator thinks of it.

Holding the cards behind his back, the mentalist seems to make an adjustment to the packet. Then he hands the packet to the spectator. The spectator thinks of a new number. Say he thinks of 3 this time. He transfers 3 cards, one at a time, from top to bottom.

Then he eliminates cards until he has one card left. This card turned over, matches the very number he thought of.

METHOD: Arrange the Ace through Ten of Spades in numerical order from Ace to Ten, Ace on top. Hand the packet to the spectator. Tell him to think of a number from 1 to 10. Whatever the number, he transfers that many from top to bottom one at a time while your back is turned.

When he's finished, take the packet from him. Square it up and secretly glimpse the bottom card as in Figure 10. The value of this card tells you the number the spectator chose. In Figure 10 the card is a 4, so you know the thought-of number was 4. Reveal the number in an impressive manner. Then fan the

Figure 10

cards with the faces toward you and cut the packet at the 6. Complete the cut so the 6 is on the bottom of the packet. You are now ready to repeat the trick but with a surprising finish.

Tell the spectator you're going to guess his number again, but this time you will make your guess before he thinks of his number. Put the packet behind your back and pretend to adjust the cards. Actually you do nothing.

Hand him the packet. Tell him to think of a number from 1 to 10 and to transfer that many cards from top to bottom. After he has done this, instruct him to eliminate cards using the following elimination shuffle.

He is to place the top card down onto the table, the next card under the packet, the next card down onto the table, the next card under the packet, and so on, until he has just one card left. The shuffle is known as a Down/Under shuffle.

When he has one card left, ask him to name the thought-of number. It might be 3. Tell him to turn up the card he holds. It will be a 3, correctly matching the thought-of number.

14. X MARKS THE SPOT

From a packet of a few cards, a spectator selects a card at random. You remark that you can draw an imaginary "X" on a table and teleport that "X" onto the back of the card selected by the spectator.

You then turn over the selected card and show that it does have a large "X" on it. Although the card is randomly chosen, it is the only card with an "X" on the back.

METHOD: Using a marking pen or a black crayon, place a large "X" on the back of a playing card. Now take 13 more cards from the deck. Place the marked card face-up so that it is eleventh from the top of the face-up packet.

Have the packet in your pocket until you want to perform this trick. Remove the packet and hold it face-up in the right hand, grasping it from above as shown in Figure 11.

Ask the spectator to name a number greater than 5, and tell him that you are going to count to his number twice. Suppose

Figure 11

he names the number 15. Take the face card with the left hand and place it on the table. Place the next card onto the table, and the next and the next. There are a total of 4 cards on the table. Count aloud, beginning with 1, as you deal the first four cards onto the table.

Now take the next card and transfer it under the packet. Transfer the next and the next, and so on, continuing the count until you reach the spectator's number—15.

Pause here and remind him that you said you would count his number twice. Now transfer cards from the back of the packet to the face one at a time, counting aloud, until you reach the spectator's number, 15. Keep the packet face-up at all times.

After you reach 15, stop and point to the face card of the face-up packet. Say, "We arrived at this card by a purely random means. I'd like to show you how an imaginary 'X' can be made to teleport to your card." Draw an imaginary "X" on

the table. Then pretend to erase it. Gather the invisible parti-
cles of the imaginary "X" and sprinkle them onto the chosen
card. Finally, turn the card over to reveal that the "X" has
materialized on the back of the card.

Note in this routine that regardless of the number named by
the spectator, you always deal the first four cards onto the table
and leave them there. Your excuse for doing this, should the
spectator ask, is that the packet was too large to begin with and
you wanted to get rid of a few cards.

15. ROYAL MIND READING

This trick combines an easy-to-do poker deal with a bit of
mind reading. The mentalist deals out two royal flushes (each
consisting of Ace, King, Queen, Jack and Ten of the same suit);
one spectator gets a royal flush in Hearts and the second spectator gets a royal flush in Spades.

Each shuffles his poker hand. Each decides on a card in his
hand and places his card in the center of the hand. The hands
are gathered, mixed, and redealt.

Despite the mixing, each spectator gets back his own royal
flush. This is the first surprise, but there is a stronger one. The
mentalist never knows the names of the two chosen cards, but
by mental powers alone he causes them to change place from
one hand to the other.

METHOD: Remove the two royal flushes and give one to each
spectator. Have each spectator shuffle his poker hand, decide
on a card, and place that card in the center or middle of the
poker hand.

When this has been done, place the first spectator's poker
hand face-down on top of the second spectator's face-down
poker hand. Say, "Before we begin, I'd like to mix the cards."

Hold the face-down packet in the left hand. Remove the top
card and place it on the bottom of the packet. Then remove the
new top card and put it on the bottom of the packet. Deal the
top five cards into a heap on the table and place (do *not* deal)
the balance of the packet on top.

This completes the mixing process. Place the complete packet
in the left hand and square up the cards. Say, "An ordinary
player might deal the cards like this." Deal out two poker

hands, a card at a time, alternating a card to the first player, then one to the second player, then one to the first player, and so on. Make sure you deal the cards into two heaps, and do not get any of the cards mixed-up or out of sequence.

Pick up the hand dealt to the first player. Turn it face-up and say, "An ordinary player might deal out a random hand like this." Turn the hand face-down and drop it on top of the other hand.

"But a mentalist uses the power of the mind to alter the arrangement of the cards. I can stack them without touching them." Pretend to concentrate, then nod as if you are satisfied that the cards have been correctly stacked.

Deal out two poker hands again, alternating cards from player to player, as before. When each player has five cards, turn up the first two cards and the last two cards of each hand, but not the center or middle card. It appears as if you have given each player his royal flush back again. It is an impressive feat, but there is an even stronger finish.

"The professional gambler can stack cards too, but this is one thing he can't do. Merely by concentrating, I'll cause the two cards you chose to change places."

Concentrate, stall to make it look hard, then turn up the center card of each hand to reveal that the first spectator's hand contains the second spectator's card and vice versa.

16. JOKER POKER

This is a good follow-up to "Royal Mind Reading" because it uses the poker theme but in a different way, demonstrating that mentalists do not play poker the way ordinary mortals do. They place a spell on one card and then let the card do all the work.

To illustrate, the mentalist hands a spectator a small packet of cards. The spectator inserts the Joker face-up into the face-down packet. Then he cuts the packet and completes the cut. He may cut as often as he desires.

Now the spectator deals out three poker hands. He deals from left to right, a card at a time, until each hand has five cards. The hand with the face-up Joker is the mentalist's poker hand.

Each of the other two hands is now shown. Each hand may contain two pair. The only thing that beats two pair is three of a kind. The mentalist calls attention to his own poker hand. He pushes out the face-up Joker and the card on either side of it.

"The Joker is wild," the mentalist says, "and it is also hexed. It attracted two cards to it, one on either side." The mentalist turns over the card on either side of the Joker to reveal for example a pair of fives. This pair, taken with the Joker, gives the mentalist three of a kind, just what he needed to beat the other players.

METHOD: Arrange three groups of Ace through Five in order, as follows: A-2-3-4-5-A-2-3-4-5-A-2-3-4-5. Suits do not matter. This is the only preparation and it can be done in front of the spectator as long as the spectator doesn't see exactly which cards you are setting up.

The spectator can cut this 15-card packet and complete the cut as often as he likes. When he is satisfied, have him insert the face-up Joker into the face-down packet. After he does this he can cut the packet and complete the cut. He may cut the packet as often as he likes, but he must end up with the Joker in the approximate center of the packet. Oddly enough, the trick won't work if the Joker is near the top or bottom of the packet.

Have the spectator drop the packet on top of the deck. Before he deals explain that the hand with the Joker will be the mentalist's hand. He then deals out three poker hands. The hand with the Joker is the mentalist's hand. The card on either side of the Joker will always form a matching pair, and the mentalist will always win with three of a kind.

⸙ 17. MENTALIST'S DREAM

One of the most effective tricks you can do is to predict what someone will do before they do it. In this demonstration you use two decks of cards. A spectator chooses a card in one deck, say the Four of Clubs. He then removes the other deck from its case, spreads it on the table, and finds that there is one (and only one) reversed card in this deck, and that it is the Four of Clubs.

METHOD: Use two decks with backs of contrasting colors. Usually you can obtain a set of two bridge decks, one red-backed and the other blue-backed. In one deck, remove the Four of Clubs, turn it over so it is face-up, and insert it into the middle of the deck. Return this deck to its case and close the flap. Place this deck aside.

Find the Four of Clubs in the other deck and place it 10th from the top of this deck. Put this deck in its case. This is the deck the spectator will use to choose a card, so remember the color of this deck. We'll assume it is the blue-backed deck.

To perform the trick, toss both decks on the table. Tell the spectator that a card will be selected in a random manner. Ask him to think of a number between 10 and 20.

As you talk, remove the blue-backed deck from its case. Place the deck in your left hand, face-down, ready to deal. Ask the spectator for his number. It may be 16.

Slowly deal 16 cards off the top of the blue-backed deck, one at a time into a pile on the table. When you have dealt 16 cards, put the rest of the deck aside.

Pick up the 16-card packet. Tell the spectator, "To further randomize your selection, we'll use the two digits in your number. The number 16 has two digits, 1 and 6. If we add them together, we get 7."

Deal 7 cards off the top of the 16-card packet. Turn up the last card dealt, saying, "This will be your card." The card is the Four of Clubs.

Now have the spectator remove the other deck from its case. He spreads the deck, face-up, on the table and finds a reversed card in the center. Turning it over, he will find it is the Four of Clubs, exactly matching the card he chose from the other deck.

Although the above example assumed that the spectator would name the number 16, the trick will work with any number between 10 and 20. Just count off a packet equal to the given number, then add together the digits of the number and count that many cards off the packet. The last card dealt will always be the Four of Clubs.

18. LETTER PERFECT

A spectator is handed a packet of cards from any deck. He is asked to think of a word and write it down, one letter on each card.

When he's done this, he shuffles or mixes the cards. Then he chooses one card, notes the card and the letter he wrote on it.

This card is returned to the packet. The packet is shuffled by another spectator.

Under these impossible circumstances the mentalist glances over the cards and immediately reveals the letter chosen by the spectator. No questions are asked. There are no gimmicks. The spectator can write any word and he can choose any letter. Yet the mentalist is always correct.

METHOD: This routine introduces the concept of one-way cards. The one-way principle is the basis for many stunning tricks in mental magic. Some decks are printed one way, but for the purpose of this trick, a group of cards from any deck will be converted to one-way cards by a subtle means.

The term "one-way" means that cards have some design feature which is either right-side up or upside down. If you look at the face of the Two of Diamonds for example, you will see that the face has no such design feature; the face of the Two of Diamonds looks the same no matter which way you turn the card. But if you write a letter of the alphabet on the Two of Diamonds, then clearly this letter can be right-side up or (if the card is turned around end-for-end) upside down. This is the key to the method used in this trick.

Tell the spectator you'd like him to think of a five-letter word. Remove five cards from the deck. They can be any five cards, but you should use low-value cards so that the spectator has plenty of white space on the face of each card for the writing.

Ask the spectator to jot down one letter of his word on each card. He is to write each letter at the *top* of each card. The result may look like Figure 12. When he has finished writing, have him shuffle the five cards.

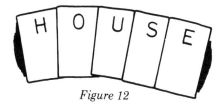

Figure 12

Take the packet from him. Hold it face-down and have him remove a card, Figure 13. As soon as he does this, hand the packet to another spectator as shown in Figure 14. This

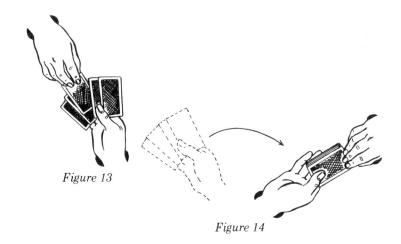

Figure 13

Figure 14

innocent-seeming gesture has the effect of turning the packet end for end. It is the ingenious idea of Theodore Annemann.

The spectator who chose a card remembers the card and the letter on it. He replaces it in the packet held by the second spectator. The spectator who holds the packet now shuffles or mixes the cards. When he's satisfied that the cards are well mixed, take back the packet from him.

Fan the cards with the faces toward you. Your goal at this point is to try to guess the chosen word. This is not difficult because the word is a short word. But your real task is even easier. On four of the cards the letters will be right-side up. On one card the letter will be upside down. This one card that is out of alignment with respect to the others is the one containing the chosen letter.

Remark that you think the word is HOUSE, or whatever it happens to be. The spectator acknowledges that you are correct. Then add, "If you chose the word House, then you are probably thinking of the letter . . . " Pause here for heightened dramatic effect, then go on to reveal which letter the spectator chose.

19. FUTURE VISION

On occasion you will be asked to demonstrate mind-reading abilities when you are not prepared. If a deck of cards is handy, you can perform an excellent test of prophetic ability. The following is a streamlined handling of a strong trick devised by J. G. Thompson, Jr.

A well-shuffled deck of cards is borrowed. The mentalist looks through the deck, then, after careful consideration, decides on two cards. He closes up the deck and places it face-down on the table.

On a piece of paper the mentalist writes the name of one of the cards on one side and the name of the other card on the other side of the paper. He then folds the paper in half.

The spectator is asked to insert the folded prediction paper into the deck at any point. He has a completely free choice of where the paper goes. After he's done this, the card directly above the slip of paper and the card directly below the paper are examined. One card may be the Five of Clubs and the other the Seven of Diamonds.

The spectator now opens the prediction slip and finds that the mentalist correctly predicted that the Five of Clubs and the Seven of Diamonds would be selected. Remember that the trick is done with a borrowed, shuffled deck. It is an outstanding mystery.

METHOD: When the deck is brought to you, make sure the spectator shuffles and cuts it to his satisfaction. Then pick up the deck and fan the cards with the faces toward you.

Pretend to study the faces of the cards, as if trying to guess where in the pack the spectator will insert the paper. What you really do is this; secretly note the top and bottom card of the deck. We'll assume they are the Five of Clubs and the Seven of Diamonds.

Close up the deck, turn it face-down and place it on the table. Make sure no one has a chance to see the face of any card as you do this. Then pick up the slip of paper. Write Five of Clubs on one side and Seven of Diamonds on the other. Fold the slip in half and in half again, so that it is no larger than the cards.

Ask the spectator to lift off some cards from the top of the deck and drop the slip in, Figure 15. Ask him if he is satisfied with this choice. If he isn't, he can change his mind.

When the spectator is satisfied that the slip of paper is at a location in the deck that no one could possibly have guessed at previously, pick up the deck and place it in the left hand.

Now spread the cards from left to right until you come to the

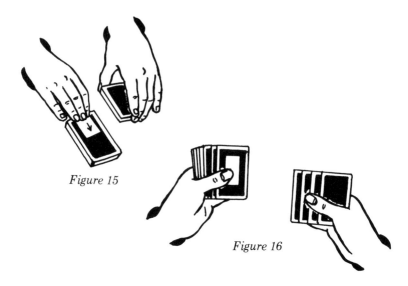

Figure 15

Figure 16

prediction. The right hand takes all of the cards above the prediction, Figure 16, and places them on the table.

The right hand then takes the folded prediction. Say to the
spectator, "Did you happen to see what I wrote on either side of
the paper?" Regardless of his reply, place the folded slip of
paper on top of the pile of cards on the table.

Now your right hand takes the remainder of the deck from
your left hand and places it on top of the cards on the table. It
appears as if the prediction is still in the same spot in the deck
that the spectator chose, but actually you've shifted things
around so that now the slip of paper is between the two cards
you've predicted.

Review the facts that you used a borrowed deck which the
spectator himself shuffled, that you never saw the deck before,
that even the slip of paper and the pencil were borrowed, and
finally that the spectator inserted the slip of paper anywhere in
the deck.

Have the spectator carefully remove the prediction slip, plus
the card above it and the card below it. When he opens the prediction, he will find that you correctly predicted the exact spot
in the deck where he would place the slip of paper.

MIND OVER MATTER

If you tell someone you would like to show him a magic trick, he will probably tell you that he knows how it's done. But if you say you want to demonstrate a mental test, the spectator will never say that he knows how it's done. The reason is that the average person thinks that mental magic is not accomplished by sleights or gimmicks, but by genuine magic or psychic powers.

The tests in this chapter will reinforce the belief that you have special abilities. You will learn the secret of causing a coin to become self-animated, of how to influence a magnetic compass, and, at the close of the chapter, how to cause a borrowed dollar bill to teleport inside a sealed envelope. The material is varied enough and strong enough to form an act in itself.

20. MONEY MENTAL

Some routines embody important basic principles in mental magic. After you learn such tricks it is wise to consider other ways the principles can be exploited. This is one such trick. Although the effect is simple, the method suggests many other tricks you can accomplish.

Three people are asked to assist. One removes a dollar bill from his pocket, crumples it up into a ball and holds it in his closed fist. The second spectator hides a crumpled five-dollar bill in his closed fist. The third spectator hides a crumpled ten-dollar bill in his closed fist.

You now put on a blindfold so that you can see nothing. Any one of the three spectators now steps forward and extends the hand holding the crumpled bill.

Of course you don't know which spectator this is, yet you are able to tell him whether he holds the dollar, the five-spot, or the ten-dollar bill in his closed fist. Further, you are able able to repeat the test with each of the other two spectators, telling each which bill he holds.

METHOD: This trick introduces a fundamental principle in blindfold work. With a handkerchief tied so as to act like a blindfold, you will find that you can see downward, as shown in Figure 17.

Figure 17

Knowing this, it still does not seem obvious how this fact would allow you to tell which bill a spectator holds, because you never see the bill. In fact it is not necessary to see the bill. You don't have to. The secret lies in an ingenious idea that does not involve the bill at all. It involves the spectator's shoes.

When each spectator removes a bill from his wallet and crumples it up, simply note the style and color of each person's shoes. Now when you are blindfolded and a spectator steps up in front of you holding a hidden bill, look down the blindfold and note his shoes.

It's unlikely that two people will be wearing exactly the same style and color shoes, so the shoes tell you who is standing in front of you. You now know the spectator. Mentally recall which bill he crumpled and held in his hand. Then go on to dramatically reveal the identity of the bill he holds. Do this with each of the three spectators.

The trick does not have to be done with bills. One spectator can conceal a ring in his hand, another a coin, and the third a key. After you note which object is held by which spectator, put on a blindfold. Have any spectator stand in front of you. Act as if you are trying to intercept his thought waves. Then go on to reveal the object he holds in his closed fist. Repeat with the other two spectators. You can present this routine either as a demonstration in mind reading or an experiment in x-ray vision.

The basic principle works extremely well with colors. Hand each of three people a different color piece of paper. Ask each person to crumple up the paper he holds. Note who gets which color. Then put on a blindfold. Have any spectator step forward and hand you his piece of paper. Hold the paper at arm's length or above your head or even behind your back. Feel the texture of the paper. State that you have developed a sense of touch so sensitive that it can detect color.

When the spectator stepped before you to hand you the paper, you looked down the blindfold. Knowing the shoe style, you know the spectator who is standing before you. From this you automatically know what color his piece of paper is.

Reveal the color of the paper, then reveal the color of each of the other pieces of paper as they are handed to you. The trick is impressive because all attention is on the color of the paper. This tends to distract attention away from any clue as to how you really know the colors.

21. THINGS EQUAL

A small box of matches is the apparatus in this impressive mystery. The spectator takes some matches and puts some back into the match box. It is found that the number of matches he holds is exactly equal to the number inside the matchbox.

To rule out the possibility of luck or coincidence, the trick is repeated, but with a difference. The spectator holds some matches and he puts some into the matchbox. But this time he knows that there are more matches in his hand than in the matchbox. The mentalist concentrates for a moment, explaining that he will try to cause the matches inside the matchbox to multiply so that once more they equal the number held by the spectator.

After a moment of concentration the mentalist opens the matchbox. Now there are exactly as many matches inside the matchbox as are held by the spectator.

METHOD: Secretly wedge two matches between the tray and the lid of the matchbox as shown in Figure 18. The number of matches in the matchbox is not essential but there should be about 20 matches. (Decorative matchboxes can be obtained in novelty and gift shops. Pick out one that looks exotic.)

Figure 18

To present the trick, open the box about halfway, Figure 18, and dump out the loose matches. Do not reveal the two matches still wedged between the tray and the lid.

Of the matches on the table, tell the spectator to take some in his left hand and an equal number in his right hand. Look away while he does this so it is clear that you don't know how many matches he has in either hand.

When he has placed an equal number of matches in each hand, take four matches of those remaining on the table. Put them into the tray.

You do not know the number of matches the spectator holds in each hand, nor do you have to. Ask him to transfer three matches from his left hand to his right hand. When he has done this, have him transfer one match from his right hand to his left hand.

Now ask him to put all of the matches from his left hand into the tray. Then tell him to count the number of matches in his right hand. The number may be eight. Tell him to count the number of matches in the matchbox and he will discover that the matchbox holds exactly the same number—eight matches.

You now repeat the trick and add a new magical element. Dump all the matches out of the tray and have the spectator add all the matches from his right hand to those on the table. Now you start again. Tell him to take some matches in his left hand and an equal number into his right hand. Look away while he does this.

When he has an equal number of matches in each hand, ask him to transfer three matches from his left hand to his right hand.

This done, pretend to concentrate. Ask a question that will distract the spectator's attention, for example, "Are you left-handed or right-handed?" This question means nothing but it will bother the spectator because he'll try to relate it to the trick. Whatever his answer, pretend to mull it over, then say,

"Transfer two matches from your right hand to your left hand."

Finally, tell him to place the matches from his left hand into the tray of the matchbox. Now turn around and close the matchbox. This will secretly add the two concealed matches to those the spectator placed into the matchbox. In other words, the two hidden matches will dislodge and fall into the tray to join the matches already there.

Ask him to count the number of matches in his hand. Both he and you know that he put fewer matches into the matchbox. Pretend to concentrate, explain that you will try to cause the matches inside the matchbox to multiply, then pick up the box and rattle it a bit.

Have the spectator open the matchbox and verify that the number of matches inside the box mysteriously increased so that now they equal the number of matches in his hand.

22. KATCH KOIN

Some of the best mental effects are done under seemingly impromptu conditions. The following trick is a bit of business that can be used when you are working for a single spectator and want to astound him with a curious feat of apparent psi power.

Ask him to remove the change from his pocket and hold it in his outstretched left hand. You then grip his left wrist with your right hand.

From your left pocket you remove an odd-looking coin. Hold it between the left thumb and forefinger. Tell the spectator to firmly grasp your left wrist with his right hand. The situation is shown in Figure 19.

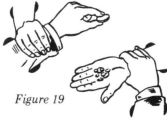

Figure 19

Tell him you're going to test his reflexes. You intend to drop the odd coin into his left hand. When he hears the coin hit the handful of change in his left hand, he is to *immediately* close his left hand into a fist to trap the odd coin.

To make the test a fair one, the spectator is asked to close his eyes during the reflex test. The mentalist adds that the spectator must be quick because the odd coin has psychic power and will try to bounce back into the mentalist's hand if the spectator isn't quick enough.

The spectator closes his eyes. The mentalist releases the odd coin, allowing it to drop. The spectator feels the coin hit his hand and *instantly* closes it around the coin. Yet when he opens his eyes, he discovers that he wasn't quick enough. The coin has escaped his grip and jumped back up into the mentalist's left hand.

The coin may be examined before and after. It can even be marked by the spectator because there is only one odd coin. There is nothing to find because there are no gimmicks. Read the above description again. See if you can detect any possible method that would account for this effect. Then read the secret to see if you were right.

METHOD: Remember that the trick must be done when you are working for one spectator only. If you do the trick with others around, they will see exactly how it works.

The secret is that before performing the trick, secretly remove a penny from your pocket. While you idly scratch your head, leave the penny on top of your head.

You're now ready to perform the trick. Proceed up to the point shown in Figure 19. When the spectator closes his eyes, your left hand makes a slight movement as if to drop the odd coin. Don't actually release the coin. Instead, tip your head forward. The penny drops into the spectator's left hand. He hears and feels a coin land in his hand and thinks it's the odd coin.

Immediately he closes his left hand into a fist. The coins in his left hand are thus automatically redistributed or mixed around and your penny gets lost among the other coins.

When he opens his eyes, however soon afterward, he is usually startled to find that the odd coin has jumped back into your left hand. The trick can be done with a ring, a charm or any unusual object. Don't use a dime or a nickel because this kills the idea of a unique, curious amulet possessed of the marvelous power to jump instantaneously back to your hand. The only other point to remember is that you should not do the trick for someone taller than you because he will spot the coin resting on the top of your head.

23. PSYCHIC COMPASS

For years the secret of this trick was closely guarded by a few psychics. It is associated with the mentalist Henry Slade, although others have used the idea to reap publicity. If you don't know the actual method involved, the demonstration seems to be impossible.

Everyone knows that a compass is influenced by the magnetic lines of force around the earth. By psychic means you can interrupt these magnetic lines and cause the compass needle to move away from true north.

To perform the test, have someone place a compass on the table. Wait for the needle to stop moving. Make sure there are no iron or steel objects nearby because you don't want anything to influence the compass needle.

There are people on either side of you, watching for any signs of trickery. Your hands are empty, your sleeves are rolled up. You place one hand palm down about six inches above the compass. Nothing happens at first, then, very slowly, the compass needle begins to move, gradually rotating away from true north.

You remove your hand and the compass needle slowly swings back to its original position.

METHOD: If people are watching intently, as they will be in this trick, it is usually not possible to get away with a trick using a palmed gimmick. The test should appear as fair as possible. That is the case here. Your hands are empty and you can wear a short-sleeved shirt because there is nothing in your hands or up your sleeves.

Use a small magnet, obtainable in a toy or department store. The magnet does not have to be large or particularly powerful because its magnetic field, however weak, is usually enough to influence the delicately balanced compass needle.

Since the magnet cannot be palmed in the hand or hidden in the sleeve, and because you can expect to be searched if someone suspects trickery, where can the magnet be safely hidden? This question was answered in a subtle way by Slade; it is hidden in your shoe, Figure 20.

Prior to performance, slip off the shoe, put the magnet inside, then put the shoe back on. The magnet is situated in the toe of the shoe. When ready to perform, sit at the table with both feet

Figure 20

Figure 21

on the floor. Have someone bring a compass to the table. Tell him to put the compass on the table directly in front of you.

Now cross the legs under the table as shown in Figure 21. This has the result of bringing the magnet under the table to a position directly below the compass.

As the magnet is brought closer to the compass, the compass needle will begin to rotate. The movement you make with the concealed magnet should be gradual. The audience will be astounded by any movement of the compass needle, so work slowly, with plenty of pauses.

You have plenty of time because no one will suspect a magnet in the shoe. They will focus their attention on your hand, which rests palm down over the compass. Since the hand is the only thing they can *see* near the compass, it is the only thing they can suspect. As in all good psychic tricks, the item under suspicion is the one thing not connected with the trick. This secret, properly exploited, can give you a considerable reputation as a psychic.

24. FIRE POWER

If you are asked to repeat the psychic compass test and do not have a magnet with which to perform the trick, you can use the following method. A good-quality compass is required. Anyone can supply it because there are no gimmicks.

Also needed is a borrowed pack of matches. When ready to perform the demonstration, have the compass placed on the table. Wait for the compass needle to stabilize.

Explaining that the energy from a common match can be intensified by psychic means to disrupt the earth's magnetic field, you light a match and hold it near the compass as shown in Figure 22.

Figure 22

Oddly enough, as the flaming match nears the compass, the audience sees the compass needle begin to fluctuate. It is a strange sight and completely beyond scientific explanation.

METHOD: The secret is well hidden. In fact it has already been given in Figure 22, but most people are unlikely to discover the principle at work.

The secret is that iron or steel can influence a compass needle just as a magnet does. The iron or steel is handed to you when the spectator hands you the packet of matches. In all match packets the match segment is fastened to the cover by a staple. The staple is either iron or steel.

Thus, when the lit match and the match packet are brought near the compass, the steel staple disrupts the magnetic field and causes the compass needle to deflect. All attention is on the match flame, so no one realizes that the staple is the cause of the mystery.

❦ 25. REPLICA

In this routine a coin chosen by a spectator produces a replica of itself. It introduces a useful concept in mental work, that of the so-called magician's choice.

Of three coins on the table, a dime, a penny, and a quarter, a spectator chooses one. This coin is placed in an envelope. The envelope is given a shake. When the envelope is opened, there are now *two* coins, the original one plus a duplicate.

Except for a written instruction given to the spectator at the start of the trick, the only apparatus is that described above, the coins and the envelope, plus two slips of paper.

METHOD: The basic method is that of the magician's choice. In other words, the spectator thinks he has a free choice of coins, but he ends up choosing the coin the mentalist wants him to choose. The novel angle in this routine is that the magician's choice is given in writing.

You will need two blank cards or two slips of paper. The wording on slip No. 1 and slip No. 2 is as given in Figure 23.

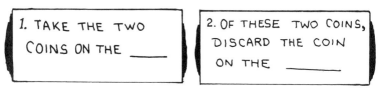

Figure 23

Note that there is a blank space on each card for a word. These words will be filled in by the spectator.

Also needed is a small envelope. An end-opening envelope, sometimes called a pay envelope or coin envelope, is convenient. You will need a dime, a quarter, and two pennies. The pennies must have the same date and must look the same.

Place one penny into the envelope so that it is positioned in a corner of the envelope as shown in Figure 24. Now drop the other three coins into the envelope so they are positioned in the opposite corner. Place the two slips of paper in the envelope. Carry the envelope in your wallet or pocket so you will be ready to do the trick at any time.

To perform, take the envelope from your pocket. Remove the two slips of paper from the envelope and place them in front of the spectator. Then grasp the envelope at the corner that holds the extra penny, tip the envelope, and let the other three coins fall out, Figure 25.

Place the envelope down on the table. The audience assumes the envelope held nothing more than the three coins and the two slips of paper. They now think the envelope is empty.

Take the three coins and arrange them in a row on the table, in front of the spectator. The penny must be the center coin.

Figure 24

Figure 25

Explain to the spectator that he is going to fill out the two slips of paper. He will then follow the instructions they indicate. He is to write the word "left" on both slips, or he can write the word "right" on both slips. It doesn't matter as long as he writes the same word on both slips in the blank space.

We'll assume he jots down the word "left" on both slips. Now tell him to follow the instruction on the first slip (the one with the number 1 on it). In our example he would take the two coins on the left. This means that he has eliminated the coin on the right. Remove the coin on the right and pocket it.

There are now two coins remaining on the table. The spectator follows the second written instruction (the slip numbered 2) and discards the coin on the left. Now there is only one coin remaining and it is the penny. It will always be the penny thanks to the magician's force.

Take the penny and drop it into the envelope. Remark that, if isolated in a place where the light is blocked out, a penny can produce a duplicate of itself. This is the "twin" principle in psychic work.

Shake the envelope. The spectator can hear two coins clink inside. Allow the first penny to slide out. Pause for dramatic effect, then allow the second penny to slide out into sight. From the audience's view, a freely chosen coin has produced a replica of itself.

26. LIGHTNING ADDITION

Because mentalists claim supernormal powers, it is logical to suppose they can perform *any* mental exercise faster than ordinary mortals. A case in point is the problem of adding a group of four-digit numbers faster than it can be done by a computer.

Here is a test that fills the bill nicely. You display several strips of cardboard or posterboard. Each strip contains a column of numbers on the front and a different column of numbers on the back, Figure 26.

The spectator mixes the four strips and arranges them on a stand as shown in Figure 27. He can use the front or back column of numbers on any strip, so obviously there are many possibilities.

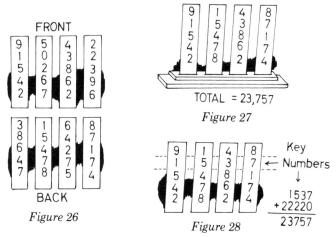

FRONT

Figure 26

BACK

Figure 26

TOTAL = 23,757

Figure 27

Key
Numbers
↓
1537
+22220
23757

Figure 28

The spectator has thus arrived at four numbers running horizontally, each with four digits. In Figure 28 the four-digit number in the top row, reading across, would be 9,148. The number in the next row would be 1,537. The other numbers would be 5,481, 4,767, and 2,824.

The mentalist picks up a pad and pencil. Hardly glancing at the four numbers, he jots something down on the pad. It is done instantly. The spectator, starting at the same time and using a pocket calculator, tries to add the four numbers as quickly as he can. No matter how fast he is, the mentalist is faster.

When the spectator announces the total, the mentalist turns the pad around and shows that he got the same total. He did it as fast as he could write, and he beat the computer.

METHOD: Needed are four strips of cardboard. Fill in the front and back of each strip as shown in Figure 26. Aside from this, you will need a simple stand to hold the four strips.

This accounts for the props. The secret to the lightning addition is direct and simple. It requires no mathematical ability on your part except the ability to add two numbers together. This is what you do.

While the spectator places the four cardboard strips into the stand, pick up the pad and write the number 22220 on it. When the spectator has completed putting the strips in the stand, turn around and glance at the *second* row of figures, Figure 28. In our example the second row is 1,537.

Jot down 1537 under 22220 and add the two numbers. The total is the total of the five four-digit numbers in the stand. You can see that the total can be arrived at instantly, just as quickly as you can write down the numbers.

This is all there is to it. All you need do now is have the spectator add the five numbers with a pocket calculator and call out the total he gets. You will have arrived at the same total long before. From your point of view the math is so simple that you can always beat the computer, but don't make it look too simple. Properly presented this is a knockout routine.

⍝ 27. LONG DIVISION

Here is one more test that will make you look like a mathematical wizard. It is based on a little-known secret. Tell a spectator that you would like him to jot down a long number, say a number with 20 digits in it. Your claim is that merely by glancing at the number you can tell if the number is exactly divisible by 4. If it isn't, you will add a couple of digits to it so that it will be exactly divisible by 4.

The spectator jots down a random number like 5764538-9763402094333. You glance at it, shake your head and say, "It isn't divisible by 4. But I can change it so it is." Now you add two more digits, a 2 and an 8, to the right end of the number.

The new number is 5764538976340209433328. When the spectator divides this number by 4, he discovers (after lengthy effort) that it is indeed evenly divisible by 4. The fact that it takes the spectator a long time to verify you claim makes your mathematical ability that much more amazing.

METHOD: Like all the best mental tricks, this one is extremely simple. No matter which number the spectator writes, no matter how long it is, no matter which digits it contains, simply add

28 to the right end of the number and it will be evenly divisible by 4.

Do not repeat the trick. Done once it is enormously impressive and you will be credited with tremendous ability at figuring long division in your head.

28. TELEPORTATION

Beyond doubt this is one of the most startling tricks you can perform. All you need is a sealed envelope. The other props are borrowed. There are no gimmicks, and as long as the sealed envelope is available, the trick can be done at a moment's notice. It is not likely to be forgotten.

Here's what it looks like. Someone signs the sealed envelope front and back to prevent switches. He can examine the seal to verify that it is genuine. He can even sign his name across the flap to make sure the seal won't be tampered with.

You borrow two dollar bills. You tear them in half, then give half of one bill to the first spectator, and half of the other bill to the second spectator. Each spectator now holds half of his own dollar bill.

Remember that each spectator holds half of his own bill. You take the other half of each bill in one hand and the envelope in the other. You place them behind your back for a second, then you bring the sealed envelope out into view.

Although the seal on the envelope has not been broken, you have caused the two halves of the borrowed bills to teleport inside the *sealed* envelope. The spectator can examine the envelope microscopically because there is nothing to find. The seal is intact. The envelope is not gimmicked.

You open the envelope and remove another sealed envelope. You open this envelope and remove one half of a dollar bill. This half-bill is given to the first spectator and it matches the half-bill he has held in view from the beginning. The other spectator then reaches into the envelope, removes the remaining half-bill and matches it up with the half-bill he has held since the beginning of the trick.

This routine has a stunning impact. The secret is little known even among magicians. Keep this trick in reserve for just the right occasion because it is devastating.

METHOD: The trick is easy to perform but you must pay attention to the details to insure success. Follow the step-by-step handling with apparatus in hand and you will have no trouble following the diabolical thinking in this method.

In preparation, take a dollar bill, tear it in half, and place the two halves in an envelope. Seal the envelope, then double seal it by placing tape along the flap. Now place this envelope inside a larger envelope. Seal the large envelope. This completes the preparation. Simply carry this large envelope with you and you are always ready to perform this trick.

To present the routine, remove the envelope from your pocket. Hand it to a spectator and ask him to inspect it and make sure it is completely sealed. If he likes, he can place adhesive tape across the flap. Ask him to sign the envelope front and back and to also sign his name across the flap.

When has has done this, take back the envelope and place it on the table. Now ask each of two spectators to lend you a dollar bill. Take the two bills, hold them together and tear in half, Figure 29.

Each hand holds two half-bills. The right hand turns palm-down and places its two half-bills on top of the two half-bills in the left hand, Figure 30.

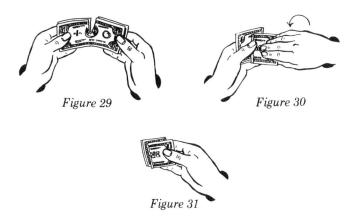

Figure 29

Figure 30

Figure 31

Walk over to the spectator on the right. Give him the topmost half-bill and tell him to hold it in full view. Then go over to the spectator on the left. Grasp the packet of three half-bills between the right thumb and first finger, Figure 31, and turn the stack over. Replace the stack in the left hand. Then hand the spectator on the left the topmost half-bill of the stack, and say, "Here's half of your bill."

It appears as if each spectator got half of his own dollar bill. But this is not so. If you followed the above procedure correctly, each spectator got back half of the *same* bill. In other words, the half-bill held by the first spectator matches the half-bill held by the second spectator.

You hold two half-bills in your left hand. Pick up the sealed envelope in your right hand. Tell the audience you will try to teleport the two half-bills into the sealed envelope.

Place both hands behind your back. As soon as they are out of sight, the left hand folds its two half-bills and stuffs them into the right jacket sleeve.

Immediately both hands come out into view again. The envelope rests on your right palm. Announce that you have caused the two borrowed half-bills to teleport inside the sealed envelope. The audience will doubt your word, thinking that the two half-bills are under the sealed envelope.

Slowly lift the envelope from your hand. Show it on both sides. Give the envelope to someone and ask him to verify that the seal is still intact and that there are no tears or holes in the envelope.

Take back the envelope. Tear off the end and allow the inner sealed envelope to slide out. Toss the large envelope onto the table. You are holding just the small envelope. Show it on both sides to emphasize that it is securely sealed.

Tear off the end of this envelope. Remove one of the half-bills, then toss the envelope onto the table. The envelope still contains a half-bill, but you will not touch the envelope again.

Walk up to the spectator on the right. Say, "This is one of the pieces I teleported into the envelope. Let's see if it matches yours." Take the half-bill he holds and place it next to the half-bill you took from the envelope, as if trying to match the pieces along the torn edge.

They won't match. You hand him back a half-bill, but not the one you took from him. Instead, you hand him back the half-bill you took out of the envelope.

When you've done this, you still hold a half-bill in your hand. Walk over to the spectator on the left. Give him the half-bill and ask him to see if it matches. To his amazement, it will.

Now, while you are still standing away from the envelope, point to the first spectator and have him remove the half-bill still inside the envelope. Tell him to hold it up to the half-bill he holds and verify that it matches. This is the strongest part of a very strong trick. The audience will remember that you never touched the half-bill still inside the envelope.

When the spectator removes the half-bill from the envelope, he will find that it does indeed match the half-bill he has been holding. You have performed an impossible trick with borrowed props, and at this point you may bow to well-deserved applause.

ꜟ BOOK TESTS

In the standard form of the book test, a spectator opens a book to a page and concentrates on a word. The mentalist, standing some distance away, reveals the word the spectator is thinking of.

This basic trick (sometimes done as a prediction) was described by writers early in this century but it was not until the 1930s that interest in book tests began to accelerate. Today there are hundreds of methods for performing book tests and the effect is considered a standard in the mentalist's repertoire.

This chapter will describe some of the best modern book tests, along with novel suggestions for presenting them.

ꜟ 29. THINK OF A WORD

This is one of the easiest book tests. By performing it several times, you will develop proficiency in the presentation of such tests. The trick has a novel presentation angle in that you do not read the spectator's mind. Instead, you read the mind of a character in the book.

A spectator is given a deck of cards. He cuts the deck and takes the two cards on top after the cut. Say these two cards are a Nine and an Eight. The mentalist does not know what the cards are. He is standing some distance away with his back turned.

The mentalist asks the spectator to add together the values of the two cards. Whatever total he gets, he opens the book to that page. In our example, the spectator got an Eight and a Nine; he would total them and arrive at 17. Then he would open the book to page 17.

The spectator is asked to look over page 17 and get a general idea of the content of the page. The mentalist then says, "I won't try to read your mind. Instead, I'll try something much more difficult. I'll try to read the mind of the major character on that page."

After a moment of concentration the mentalist says, "The character's initials are J. R. His first name is Jack. He is worried about a problem as he walks into an office building. I see him talking to a woman as he goes up the elevator."

The mentalist continues on a bit more, then comes back to the beginning as he concludes by saying, "His name is clearer. It's John Ryan, and he plans to kill his boss. You can see why I don't read detective stories. I always know the killer's identity because I can read his mind!"

Of course the spectator verifies that your description was completely correct.

METHOD: The method used here is basic to a class of book tests in which you use a known book. Although the spectator appears to have a free choice of any page, his choice is forced. He will arrive at page 17, no matter which two cards he chooses from the deck.

Before the performance, place the Eight of Hearts and the Nine of Spades on top of the deck. Decide on a book you want to use. It should be a book with a dramatic plot so that you can weave an interesting story into your presentation. Paperback mysteries or adventure stories are a good bet. Try to pick a popular book on the chance that many in your audience will already be familiar with the story.

When you've decided on a book, open it to page 17. Read the page carefully and remember all the important names and incidents that occur on the page. If time permits, read the entire book to find out what fate awaits the characters who appear on page 17. You don't have to remember the complete plot. Just get a general idea of the story. The only thing you have to remember in detail is the material that appears on page 17.

You are now ready to perform the trick. Place the deck of cards in front of the spectator. Invite him to cut the deck. He cuts off about half, as shown in Figure 32.

Now pick up the bottom half and place it on top of the other half, but at right angles, as shown in Figure 33.

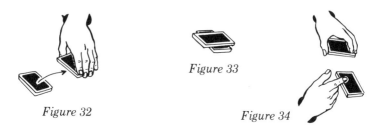

Figure 33

Figure 32

Figure 34

It is important at this point to draw attention away from the deck for a moment. The reason is that you want the spectator to forget which half of the deck is the top half and which is the bottom half. You have a natural excuse in introducing the book.

"You all know people who give you a murder mystery to read and, as they hand over the book, tell you, 'You'd never guess that the butler did it.' Mentalists have the same problem. They can read the minds of the characters in the book, so they know the killer's identity immediately. This is like being able to read the minds of people in dreams, or being able to tell a great deal about a person from a photo or portrait."

Show the book and hand it to a spectator. Now lift off the top part of the deck and point to the top of the remaining half, Figure 34. Say, "We'll use two cards to give us a random page number." Ask a spectator to remove the two cards at the point where he cut the deck. Actually the two cards he removes are the Eight of Hearts and Nine of Spades. This move is known as the Cut Force or X Force and is a standard method used to force cards.

Walk to a distant corner of the room. Ask the spectator to add together the values of the two cards, and open the book to that page. Of course the total will be 17. Once he opens the book to page 17, the rest is a question of presentation on your part. Just remember to follow the golden rule of mental work: don't make the trick look too easy.

30. THE PRINTED WORD

At first this may appear to be the same method as in the preceding trick, but it is based on an entirely different principle. With the deck in his own hands, a spectator cuts the deck anywhere and completes the cut. He takes the top two cards and totals them. Whatever the total, he opens a phone book to that page and notes the name, address and phone number of the first listing at the top of the page.

The mentalist, standing across the room with his back turned, then proceeds to reveal the chosen name, describes the location and appearance of the house, then reveals the exact address, and finally reveals the phone number of the chosen listing.

The trick seems to be a test of genuine mind-reading ability because the apparatus is out of the mentalist's hands from start to finish.

METHOD: The mentalist does not actually know the exact choice until after the spectator begins to concentrate on it. This is due to the fact that although a force is used, it can be either of two names in the phone book.

The deck is stacked to provide a force total. The stack is known in mentalism parlance as a 14-15 stack because it will force a total of either 14 or 15, depending on where the spectator cuts the deck.

From the top down, the stack is, 7-8-6-9-5-10-4-J-3-Q-2-K-A-K-2-Q-3-J-4-10-5-9-6-8-7-7-8-6, and so on until all the cards in the deck are used except two Aces, which are put in the pocket and not used. Remember that the Jack is 11, the Queen 12 and the King 13.

This subtle arrangement was marketed by H. S. Paine in 1922 and has since become a valuable force method used by mentalists.

If you use a local telephone directory, note the first name listed on page 14, and the first name on page 15. It will pay you to jot down the addresses, and then visit these homes if they are in your local area. This way you can walk by the house and find out what neighborhood it's in, the general appearance of the house, whether there are trees in front, and so on. If there's a car parked in the driveway or garage, it probably belongs to the people who live in the house. Note the make and color of the car.

To present the test, hand the deck to someone. Turn your back and walk to a far corner of the room. Ask the person to cut the deck and complete the cut. Tell him to deal the top two cards onto the table and put the balance of the deck aside.

Now direct him to pick up the two cards and total their values. He can only arrive at a total of 14 or 15, thanks to the stack. Whatever the total, he opens the book to that page. Tell him to look at the first word on the page and to concentrate intently on the name, the address, and the phone number.

There is a subtle point here that tells you whether the page is 14 or 15, and it is this. Page 14 will always be on the left, and page 15 will always be on the right. Thus, you turn briefly to ask the spectator if he's concentrating on the listing. Glance at him and simply note whether he's looking at the left-hand or right-hand page. This tells you whether he chose page 14 or page 15.

Slowly reveal the name, the appearance of the house, then the address of the house, then the phone number. Since you have described the house in some detail, the spectator may want to call the number and verify that your description is correct. This is the clincher, because when he dials the number, the party on the other end will verify every detail! (It's advisable to get permission from the party at the other end some time in advance.)

31. WORD ON THE PAGE

The above test can be enlarged, thanks to an idea of Annemann's. After the spectator has cut the deck and completed the cut, tell him to take the top and bottom card. Then have him hand the deck to another spectator. Have this person also take the top and bottom card.

Each spectator, on totaling his cards, will arrive at a different total. This strengthens the idea that the spectator could have arrived at *any* total. It appears as if there would be dozens of combinations, but in fact there are only four; 13, 14, 15, or 16.

Have the first spectator open the book to the page designated by his total and concentrate on the first listing. You can tell whether he's looking at an odd-numbered or an even-numbered page because the odd numbers are always on the right and the even-numbered pages are always on the left.

Knowing that he chose an odd number, for example, you then know this number must be either 13 or 15. From here it is a simple matter to nail down which number. For instance, if the first word on page 13 is Baylor, and the first word on page 15 is

Caldwell, say to the spectator, "I get the impression that the name is a short one. Does it begin with the letter B?" If he says yes, you know it's Baylor. Otherwise it's Caldwell.

Reveal the chosen listing. Then repeat with the second spectator. The fact that each spectator chooses a different name only makes the test stronger.

You are not limited to mysteries and phone books in these tests. Cookbooks, home-repair manuals, history books, and so on, will each suggest patter and presentation ideas to you. As a pertinent example, the following trick uses an atlas to exploit a novel presentation angle.

32. WINGED THOUGHTS

The phenomenon known as out-of-body projection allows the mind to leave the body, travel great distances, and observe events in faraway places. A demonstration of remote viewing would look like this:

A spectator is given a world atlas. Another spectator calls out any page number. There are no restrictions. Let's say he calls out page 128.

The party with the atlas opens the book to page 128 and scans the page to get a general idea of the map and the area depicted. All of this time the mentalist stands with his back turned. He never sees the book and never asks a question.

Picking up a slate and piece of chalk, the mentalist begins to draw or sketch a rough map. As he draws, he says, "I have the impression that I'm walking along a narrow dirt road. There is a mosque to my left, and beyond that a stone building with an iron balcony. Near the center of town I see a glimpse of the desert at the horizon. Someone approaches and I ask him the name of the city. He says something in a language I can't understand, but it sounds like the city is Cairo."

The spectator is asked to describe the major city depicted on the map he's chosen. The map is of Egypt and the major city is indeed Cairo.

METHOD: What makes the trick so puzzling is that the spectator can open the book to any page. You ask no questions, your back is turned, yet you begin to draw a street map immediately and eventually name the major city on the map.

First you have to have a good atlas. The slate should measure about 9 inches by 12 inches. Preparation is simple. Open the atlas to page 1 and note the general content. Pick out a prominent city and two or three important features depicted on the map, things like rivers, mountains, deserts, proximity to an ocean or other large body of water. You do not need a detailed account. Merely pick out a few important items shown on the map in the vicinity of the major city.

Jot this information down on the slate *in pencil*, beginning at the upper-left corner. If page 1 did indeed show a map of Egypt, your entry might read something like, "1-Egypt-Cairo-Suez."

If page 2 showed a map of Norway, your penciled entry on the slate would read, "2-Norway-Oslo-North Sea." Continue this way, listing the page number and the important details on each page. You will have two or three columns of information on each side of the slate. This preparation can be done rapidly, and once completed, you can use it for a number of repeat performances.

The reason for making the entries in pencil is that the written information on the slate is invisible to anyone else in the room, but up close you can easily read the entry you want. Thus, although the slate is filled with writing, it appears to be completely blank to the audience.

To perform, situate yourself at a table some distance away from the participating spectators. Have one of them pick up the atlas and look through it. Ask the other spectator to call out a page number. It can be any number as long as it is a page number in the atlas.

Say the page number is 31. The spectator holding the atlas turns to page 31. Pretend to go into a trance (there is no standard approach, but the usual procedure is to sit very quietly for a minute). Then nod your head as if your are zeroing in on the country the spectator has in mind.

Remember, you must act as if you already know the country. Then the slate is a mere incidental, a convenient way of describing what you see.

Pick up the slate and hold it in front of you. With the free hand, fumble in your pocket for a piece of chalk. You know exactly where the chalk is, but stall to allow yourself time to find the right penciled listing on the slate. You are looking for the listing on the slate next to #31, since this is the page called out by the spectator.

Once you get the proper information from the penciled listing, take out the chalk. From here if is a matter of acting. You want to make it appear that you are wandering down the street in a city far from home. It is difficult to fake this to make it sound authentic, but psychics have a useful way of faking the trance. What it comes down to is this. Recall to mind a trip you took as a child. It can be a trip to the candy store, or the route you took home from school. Describe *this* journey. Thus you are drawing from a memory, from something you already know, and your description will have an authentic ring.

Since you know the country chosen by the spectator, you can alter details to fit the chosen country. By adding features like rivers, lakes and mountains, you build up a convincing picture of your ability at remote viewing. Then go on to name the major city and have the spectator verify that you were correct.

33. THE WANT AD TEST

Book tests can also be done with magazines and newspapers. All of the principles used in the preceding tests can be applied to tricks using magazines, with no important changes in method or handling. But there are advantages in using newspapers and magazines, and methods have been devised to handle these forms of printed material. This test is an excellent example.

Before the performance, clip out a column of want ads from the classified section of your local newspaper. On a slip of paper, jot down the content of the want ad at the bottom of the column, that is, the last ad. Fold the slip of paper and seal it in an envelope. This is your prediction.

When you are ready to demonstrate the want ad test, hand the sealed envelope to a spectator for safekeeping. Hold the column of want ads in the left hand, but the column is upside down. In other words, in Figure 35 the predicted want ad is at the top of the column.

Tell the spectator that you will snip off want ads, beginning at the bottom of the column, until he calls stop. You will then

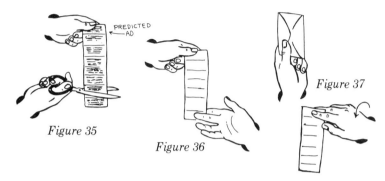

Figure 35

Figure 36

Figure 37

use whatever ad is at the bottom after your random cutting for your feat of mentalism.

Beginning at the bottom of the column, cut off half-inch strips of paper. Let the cut-off pieces flutter to the floor. At some point the spectator will call stop. When he does, put the scissors down.

Your right hand now grasps the lower part of the column of want ads, Figure 36. You then ask for the prediction envelope. As you are offered the envelope, reach for it with the left hand, Figure 37.

The result of this action is that the column of want ads has been secretly turned end for end. You now approach the spectator who called stop. Remind the audience that you cut off ads from the bottom of the column until stop was called. Then have the spectator read aloud the want ad at the bottom of the column. He thinks this is the ad he stopped you at.

After the ad is read, have him open the prediction envelope. He reads the prediction aloud and finds that it is correct.

34. STOP PRESS

Sometime when a friend calls you, ask him if he has a copy of the day's newspaper at hand. If he does, ask him to bring the paper to the phone. Tell him you don't want to know the name of the paper.

When he brings the paper to the phone, tell him that you want him to name a number. Ask how many pages the newspaper has. If 76, then tell him to name a number between 1 and 76.

Say he names 27. Instruct him to open the paper to page 27 and gaze at the overall appearance of the page. It is not necessary for him to focus his attention on any one picture or headline—you just want to get a general telepathic image of what he sees.

Then, without asking a single question, you proceed to reveal the content of the page he has chosen. In a general way you describe photos, ads, headlines, and articles. You explain that your information is not specific because it is difficult to get thoughts along telephone lines, but you *do* give him an amazingly complete description of the page he has chosen.

METHOD: If you expect a call from your friend tonight, make sure you pick up a copy of the day's newspapers on the way home. In any city there will be no more than a few large dailies and one local paper.

With the newspapers handy by the phone, wait for your friend's call. During the conversation, ask him if he has a copy of the day's paper. Tell him you don't want to know the name of the paper.

Now say, "I'd like you to think of a number between one and—by the way, how many pages are in your newspaper?" The spectator may say 76. This is the crux of the method. Almost always, two different newspapers will not have the same number of pages on a given day. So, look through the newspapers in front of you and find the one that has 76 pages. Now you know the paper that the subject is using.

If his newspaper has 76 pages, tell him to name a number between 1 and 76. If he names 27, tell him to open to page 27. Wait until you hear him leafing through the pages. This will cover any sound you make when you secretly turn to page 27 in your copy of the same newspaper.

The rest is just presentation. Although you *could* give him an exact description of the page, the effect would be too strong. You don't want him suspecting that you might have a duplicate paper, so give him a general description of the page, throw in one or two small errors, but make it clear that you are receiving a telepathic signal via the telephone as to what he is seeing.

Just one small tip to strengthen the presentation. As you reveal the general content of the page, say, "And I see a headline involving an important government—" Stop talking.

Then say, "Sorry, that headline is going to be in *tomorrow's* edition." It is a small point but one that bothers the spectator and leads him to believe that you just might be able to see the future.

35. MAGAZINE MENTALISM

The above trick was independently developed by several magicians, among them John Hudak and Leon Maguire. J. G. Thompson, Jr. devised another trick using the general principle. Here is his description of the routine.

The next time you are in the home of a friend whom you enjoy baffling, make a careful mental note of all the magazines you see lying about. At the first opportunity, purchase the ones you do not already have.

Write down the name of each, followed by the number of pages contained in each. Have the magazines near the phone and call your friend.

When he gets on the line ask him to grab a magazine and bring it to the phone. Say, "Ready? Now I want you to name a number between 1 and—by the way, how many pages does your magazine have? 70. Okay, then name a number between 1 and 70."

As soon as the number of pages is known, run your finger down the list until you come to the listing for a magazine with the same number of pages. Get the magazine from the pile and open it to the page called out by the spectator.

Now reveal in a general way the content of the chosen page. You can even be specific about certain items. For example, you can say, "I seem to get a clear mental picture of one word on the page. It's the third word in the top line and it looks like 'chair.' Is that correct?"

The advantage of this test is that magazines are published weekly or monthly, so you can buy a supply of the current week's magazines, and be able to perform the trick for three or four friends, on different days, using the same magazines.

PSYCHIC SECRETS

In this chapter you will learn the secret of spoon-bending, how to speed up a watch by psi power, and how to read the thoughts of someone who is out of the room. This chapter also introduces the idea of two-person mentalism, that is, the trick involving a mentalist and a medium. Many people suspect that two-person tricks are done by codes, but as you will learn in this chapter, the methods are far different and far more clever.

36. CRYSTAL CLEAR

Long before crystal radios plucked electric waves out of the air, mediums were using glass crystals to filter thought waves out of the ether. Crystals, or crystal balls, are obtainable in magic-supply houses. If you cannot obtain one conveniently (they are not cheap), you can use a substitute item that mediums themselves use, a glass of water.

A few paper napkins, a glass of water and a pencil are the apparatus used in this strange feat. These items are placed on a table in the next room. A spectator goes into the room alone, stares into the glass of water and focuses his thoughts. He then jots down something on the center of one of the napkins.

He gathers up the napkin so that the writing is on the inside. The crumpled napkin is given to the mentalist, who burns it in plain view, letting the ashes fall into an ashtray.

Then the mentalist goes into the next room, concentrates on the glass of water and writes something on another napkin. When he returns, he asks the spectator to describe what he wrote. After this is done, the writing on the mentalist's napkin is read aloud by anyone. The mentalist has written exactly the same thing!

METHOD: The principle at work here is a self-working version of a sleight known as the center tear. The center tear is one of the fundamental principles in mental work, as it allows you to gain instant access to anything a person writes down.

In this version, while the spectator is in the next room writing his thoughts in the center of a napkin, Figure 38, you secretly moisten the left forefinger and thumb. This is easily accomplished if there is a glass with a cold drink on the table. Moisture will condense around the outside of the drink. Simply grasp the glass as shown in Figure 39 and you will be prepared.

When you get back the crumpled napkin from the spectator, place it in the left hand as shown in Figure 40. Close the hand around the napkin. What happens is that the moisture transfers from the left hand to the napkin at a point above the spectator's writing. The moist napkin will now tear noiselessly and easily.

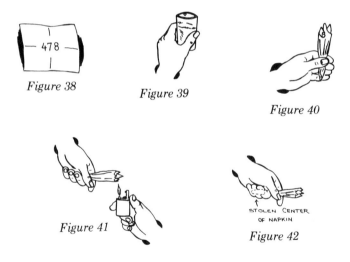

Figure 38

Figure 39

Figure 40

Figure 41

Figure 42

Don't tear the napkin yet. With the right hand, light a cigarette lighter. Bring the ends of the napkin down into the flame, Figure 41. As the flame progresses along the napkin, draw the left thumb and first finger in, grasp the napkin firmly and push it out, Figure 42. The left fingers retain the center of the napkin in the palm of the left hand, while the left fingers allow the flaming napkin to drop into the ashtray.

Say to the spectator, "Your thoughts have been transferred

from paper to air. The glass of water will act as a focal point for your thoughts."

Go into the next room. Secretly open the stolen piece of the napkin and read the spectator's writing. You may not be able to make out all of it, but you can get the general drift of his written words.

Write a similar thought on another napkin. Then reenter the room with the other guests, have the spectator describe what he wrote, then have someone else verify that you wrote the same thing.

37. TIME WILL TELL

In earlier times mentalists received prophetic information from oracles. This arrangement may have suggested the idea of the two-person trick in later centuries. In Robert-Houdin's time it was known as "second sight," and it was probably then that the two-person trick began to gain in popularity. Today such tricks are feature attractions in the mentalist's act. The following routine is a sample trick which can be performed in the living room.

A spectator removes his watch, sets it at any time setting and hands it to you behind your back. He then picks up a deck of cards, transfers cards one at a time from top to bottom, stops at any point, takes the top card and drops in into his pocket.

All of this takes place while your assistant (called a medium) has been out of the room. You hand her the deck. She concentrates for a second and then names the card the spectator has in his pocket.

Now attention is turned to the spectator's watch. Previously he set it at a time that only he knows. The medium concentrates for a moment and then proceeds to reveal the exact setting of the watch.

You never know the setting of the watch or the chosen card, and there are no codes. The trick may be done anywhere with any borrowed watch.

METHOD: You are actually doing two tricks here. One is the revelation of the card in the spectator's pocket and the other is the revelation of the setting on the watch. We'll take the card effect first.

Stack the King through Ace of Spades in order on top of the deck. The King is the top card, the Queen next, the Jack next, and so on. This is the only preparation. In the next trick we will describe a method that uses any deck and no preparation, but for the present discussion a stack will be used as described above.

Explain that your assistant can pick up thought waves. Tell the audience you will try to transmit certain thought patterns to her while she is locked in another room. Have the medium go into an adjoining room and close the door. Invite a spectator up to assist. He must be one who wears an expansion-band watch (*not* of the digital kind).

Tell him to remove his watch, reset the hands to any time, remember the setting and give you the watch behind your back.

After he has done this, tell him to pick up the deck, think of a number from 1 to 10 and transfer that many cards from top to bottom. He does this silently so that the medium in the next room cannot hear how many cards he deals from top to bottom.

While he does this, take his watch, which you are holding behind your back, and secretly slip it onto your right wrist. The face of the watch should be at the inside of the wrist.

When the spectator stops dealing, tell him to take the top card and place it in his pocket.

Take the deck from him and hold it face-up in your hand. Keep your left hand behind your back as if it still held the watch. The deck is in your right hand. Have the medium open the door. Hand her the deck claiming she must touch it. As indicated in Figure 43, she sees the bottom card of the deck and also the setting of the spectator's watch. She then returns the deck to you.

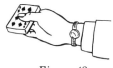

Figure 43

Knowing the bottom card, she knows that the card in the spectator's pocket is one less in value and of the same suit. If the bottom card is the Six of Spades, the card in the spectator's pocket must be the Five of Spades.

After a minute of concentration, the medium, still in the next room, slowly reveals the name of the card in the spectator's pocket, saying, "It seems to be a black card . . . a low value . . . a Five . . . Yes, I see it, the Five of Spades."

In the meantime, while all attention is on her, you place your right hand behind your back. With the aid of the left hand, the spectator's watch is slipped off the right wrist.

The medium never looks at you. Walking from the adjoining room to join the present company, she acts as if she just remembered that the spectator also set his watch at a particular time. Slowly she reveals the setting on the watch. When this has been done, remove the spectator's watch from behind your back and have him verify that the medium was right.

38. A ROOM AWAY

In this trick the medium goes into an adjoining room and closes the door. While she is out of the room, a card is chosen from a borrowed, shuffled deck. The card is returned to the deck and the deck placed in a card case.

Although the medium never asks a single question, when the deck is given to her she immediately names the chosen card. All props are borrowed. There are no gimmicks or codes, and the test appears unfathomable.

METHOD: The routine is based on an idea of Victor Marsh. After the medium goes into the adjoining room, borrow a deck of cards. When you remove the deck from the case, have someone shuffle the deck.

Ask him to remove one card and show it to the others. After he removes the card, return the balance of the deck to the case as in Figure 44.

While all attention is directed to the spectator's card, turn the card case over. Pull back the flap and hold it in place with the

Figure 44

Figure 45

forefinger. Now tell the spectator to push his card into the deck. This is shown in Figure 45. The spectator thinks his face-down card is going into the face-down deck, but because you secretly turned the card case over while no one was looking, the chosen card is going face-down into a face-up deck.

Close the flap of the card case. Hand the cased deck to a spectator and ask him to bring the deck to your medium. After she gets the deck and is alone in the room, the medium removes the deck from its case, spreads the cards and simply notes which card is reversed. She turns this card over and replaces it in the deck. Then she returns the deck to the case. Now she reveals the identity of the chosen card.

Note that this method of selecting a card can be used in the previous trick. If you decide to use the two tricks in combination, the combined ideas can be presented impromptu, with no preparation, using any deck and any watch. It makes an impressive feat of telepathy under true impromptu conditions.

39. IMPOSSIBLE ESP

What are known today as the five ESP symbols had their start in a set of symbols which were designed to be easily transmitted via thought waves. The first printed form of these symbols were known as Zenner cards. They were popularized by J. B. Rhine and other psychic investigators.

The five standard ESP symbols, plus one more, are used in this test of precognition, the ability to see events before they happen. The symbols are drawn on a list, Figure 46, and two of them are chosen by the throw of an ordinary die. The mentalist correctly guesses which symbols will be chosen before any choice is made.

METHOD: Draw up the list shown in Figure 46 on a strip of cardboard or posterboard. This can be done with a borrowed

Figure 46

file card and a marking pen on the spur of the moment, since there is nothing special about the list or the order in which the symbols are placed on it.

Aside from the list you will need a die and a teacup. Explain that you will try to see into the future and glimpse which symbols will be chosen. Pick up a slip of paper, write one of the symbols on it with the marking pen, fold the paper and place it in plain view on the table.

Have a spectator roll the die several times to satisfy himself that it's not loaded. When he's satisfied, tell him to drop the die into the teacup, shake the die around and leaving the die in the cup, see which number comes up.

As he does this, pick up the list and hold it so that only you can see the symbols. When the spectator has a number, show *him* (but no one else) the list. Have him count down from the top to the number signified by the die. For example, if he rolls a 5, have him note the fifth symbol from the top of the list, the cross.

At times you will be lucky. The symbol he chose is the symbol you wrote on the prediction paper. If so, stop the trick right here because you can't do any better. Simply have him open the prediction and verify that you were correct. The trick is so astounding that you can quit now and forever have a reputation for amazing powers.

If you aren't right, you can still bring the trick to a successful finish. Just note the symbol chosen by this spectator. Say it's the square.

Place your list writing-side down on the table. Pick up another slip of paper. Tell a second spectator that he too will choose a symbol. Pretend to see the future, then draw a picture of the square on the second slip of paper. Fold the slip and toss it over with the first slip.

Now pick up the teacup. The die is still in it. Turn the teacup over, Figure 47, allowing the die to turn over onto the table. The die isn't allowed to roll. Just allow it to turn over so the opposite

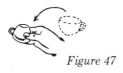

Figure 47

face is up. In our example, if the first spectator rolled a 5, the second spectator will get a 2.

Pick up the list and show it to the second spectator, but in picking it up, turn it over end for end so that it looks like Figure 48. Now, starting from the top, the second spectator counts

Figure 48

down to the symbol corresponding to the number he sees on the die, and he remembers this symbol. He is the only one to see the symbol he chose.

Fold the list of symbols and place it in your pocket. Now pick up the two prediction slips, open them and place them on the table. They must be put in view at the same time. The reason is that both spectators will see that you correctly predicted the symbol they chose, and both will react at the same instant.

This must be so because both spectators picked the same symbol. In order to make it *seem* that each slip of paper contains a correct prediction, you must therefore place them in view at the same time. Each man will see his symbol, so each will congratulate you on having extraordinary powers of mind.

✍ 40. THE INVISIBLE DIE

A deck is freely shuffled by a spectator. Then the deck is dropped into a glass. The spectator is asked to roll an invisible die and call out which number he rolls. If he looks bewildered at this request, just ask him to call out a number between 1 and 6.

Say he calls out 4. The fourth card from the top of the deck is noted by the spectator. The magician, standing some distance away with an index card and a pencil, jots down a few notes, then goes on to reveal the chosen card. Remember that the deck is freely shuffled by the spectator.

METHOD: Beforehand, remove the four Eights from the deck plus the Joker. Place the Eights on the table in order—Clubs,

Hearts, Spades, Diamonds from the top down. Then place the Joker on top of the packet. You should have a face-down packet, the top card of which is the Joker. The next card is the Eight of Clubs, the next the Eight of Hearts and so on.

You'll need a glass large enough to hold the deck of cards. Place the packet into the glass, and place an index card into the glass. The index card is slightly larger in size than a playing card. The setup is shown in Figure 49. This is the performer's view of the apparatus. The spectator sees an index card in the glass but he does not see the cards hidden behind the index card.

Figure 49

Figure 50

Hand the deck to the spectator. Have him shuffle and cut it. Then take it from him and drop it into the glass, Figure 50. Remove the file card and start to walk away, saying that you'll use the file card to record your thoughts.

What you have done is to secretly load the four Eights onto the top of the deck in a natural manner. Tell the spectator that there is an invisible die on the table. Some poeple take this seriously and will ask where the die is. You should act serious and point to a spot on the table.

Tell the spectator that a die has six numbers on it and that he is to roll the die and tell you the number that comes up. "Naturally," you add, "the number can be any number between 1 and 6."

Since the spectator is limited to a number *between* 1 and 6, he can only call out 2, 3, 4, or 5. As he goes though the motions of rolling the invisible die, tear the file card in half and write an "8" on one half. Place this on the table, writing side down. The important point, which you audience is aware of, is that you started writing before the spectator called out a number.

When he calls out a number, have him remove the deck from

the glass and count down to that number. Since his number is between 1 and 6, he must get one of the Eights.

You are still holding a piece of the file card in your hand. If the spectator called out 2, write "Clubs" on this piece of file card. If he called out 3, write "Hearts," If 4, write "Spades," and if 5, write "Diamonds." Toss this half of the file card onto the table, writing-side down.

When he's chosen his card, have him show it to the audience. Then ask him to read the prediction and he will see that it's correct.

41. THE TIME POOL

This routine is one of the most gripping psychic tests you can perform. It uses a little-known fact to produce a strange result, the apparent ability to cause watches to speed up.

A glass, covered with aluminum foil, is shown. You explain that the glass contains an odd substance which causes time to speed up or slow down. To demonstrate how it works, you place the glass in the center of the table and ask for the loan of someone's watch.

The foil wrapping is removed from the mouth of the glass. Holding the watch by the watchband, you dip the watch into the glass. The watch is then removed and placed on the table.

You comment that the substance inside the glass evaporates quickly and even now is disappearing. Then you have the spectator look at the face of the watch.

Whereas the watch face originally showed the correct time, now it has speeded up and is an hour or more ahead of the correct time.

METHOD: The watch is borrowed and the glass is just an ordinary empty drinking glass. Both the glass and the watch may be examined; there is nothing to find.

Like many of the tricks in this book, "The Time Pool" is an excellent example of how a little-known fact is exploited to produce an astounding mystery. The secret is this. The watch you borrow must be a digital watch, and the reason you must borrow this type of watch is that a digital watch will speed up when it is in the vicinity of a strong magnet.

The working should now be clear. The magnet is hidden in the toe of the shoe (just as it was for the "Psychic Compass" routine, page 35). You are seated at the table. The glass is merely an empty glass covered with metal foil. Direct all attention at the glass. Make it seem as if the glass is the important item of apparatus. You are following the psychic's standard rule; direct attention at the one object that is not linked with the method.

Remove the foil from the glass. Then borrow a digital watch. Have the spectator check the time on the watch.

Cross you legs under the table. This brings the magnet to a position directly under the tabletop. Adjust the position of the glass so that it rests on the table right above the spot where the magnet is located.

Hold the watch by the watchband, between your thumb and forefinger. Dip the watch into the glass as if dipping it into a liquid. Remove the watch, gently shake off the invisible liquid, then place the watch on the table.

Remark that the substance inside the glass, which you refer to as "bottled time," is evaporating. Then have the spectator check the setting on the watch. He'll be amazed to learn that the watch has advanced many minutes, in some cases as much as an hour.

When dipping the watch into the glass, make sure the face of the watch is away from the spectator's view. The reason is that as the watch is lowered and enters the magnetic field of the concealed magnet, the time will begin to speed up. You don't want the spectator to actually see this happening. It's stronger to wait until the end of the demonstration for him to discover that his watch has speeded up.

❀ 42. SEVEN KEYS

The lock and key effect, in which you are able to find the one key out of seven that opens a lock, was suggested by Kolar. The following routine is one of the easiest and most direct approaches to this mystery.

A spectator is given a lock and seven keys. One and only one of the keys opens the lock. The spectator tries to find the right key. It may take him a while, but eventually he finds the key that opens the lock.

This key is placed in an evelope and the envelope sealed. The other keys are tried and it is verified that none of them will open the lock. Each of these keys is then sealed in its own envelope.

The seven sealed envelopes are dropped into a paper bag and the contents mixed by the spectator. The mentalist then reaches into the bag, removes an envelope, concentrates for a moment, then tosses the envelope aside. He does this with three or four more envelopes, then he stops.

The envelope he holds in his hand is given to the spectator. The spectator opens the envelope, removes the key and tries it in the lock. It is the correct key because it opens the lock!

Note that the spectator handles the envelopes at all times. It is he who seals each key in a different envelope. Each key can go into any envelope. The spectator himself seals the envelopes, he drops them into the paper bag, and he mixes the envelopes around.

The spectator can even remove each envelope from the bag and then hand the envelope to the mentalist. Finally, it is the spectator who opens the envelope, removes the key, and verifies that the key does open the lock.

METHOD: When you purchase a lock at a hardware store, it generally comes with two keys that open it. The extra key is a spare. To prepare for this routine, buy a lock and also purchase six keys that won't open the lock. You now have a lock, two keys that open the lock, and six keys that don't.

Take the spare key that opens the lock and seal it in an envelope. Mark the envelope with a pencil dot at the upper-left and lower-right corners so you can identify the envelope later on. Then place the marked, sealed envelope at the bottom of the paper bag.

When presenting the trick, hand out the lock and the key that opens it. Also hand out seven envelopes and the six keys that don't open the lock. Let the audience try each key to satisfy themselves that only one key opens the lock.

A spectator then seals each key in an envelope. When he's done this, have him drop the envelopes into the paper bag.

Have him mix up the contents of the bag, reach into the bag and take out an envelope.

Place the envelope to your forehead, pretend to concentrate, then toss the envelope aside. Continue wth the other envelopes as they are handed to you. Sooner or later you will be handed the marked envelope. Concentrate, nod your head, toss this envelope to the spectator.

Have the spectator tear open this envelope and try the key in the lock. It works, the lock opens, and the trick is complete. The spectator has no reason to open each of the other envelopes and try each key in the lock because he has already done this at the beginning of the trick.

43. KEY-RECT

This is another version of the lock and key trick that is ideal when performing at a friend's home. Borrow his house key and drop it into an envelope that you've secretly marked. Then (with his consent) have him step outside the house. Close the door and lock him out.

Borrow five or six more keys and have each sealed in an envelope. Gather the envelopes, including the marked envelope and have them mixed. Then hold each envelope up to your forehead as you pretend to try to guess which envelope has the correct key.

Eventually pick up the marked envelope, remark that this is the correct one, tear it open and remove the key. Have someone slip the key under the door to the host who is on the other side. He tries the key in the lock and opens it. It's an amusing presentation and one that will be remembered.

44. PSILVER

"Psi" is a term used by psychic researchers to denote the power of the mind over inanimate objects. The ability to cause a pencil to move or a ring to break is a subject of great interest. In the following routine the mentalist uses common objects (a spoon and a fork) to produce a decidedly uncommon result.

Like "Katch Koin" (page 33), this routine is intended for

performance before a single spectator. It is actually a series of three different tricks. While sitting across the table from a friend in a restaurant, offer to show him a curious experiment in the supernatural.

Taking out a pad and pencil, you jot down a prediction. Then you fold the paper and toss it onto the table in front of the spectator. Now you borrow his fork and spoon, place them under the table and mix them up a bit. Tell him to name one of the utensils without looking.

He does. Say he picks the spoon. He opens the prediction and reads, "You will choose the spoon."

You're still holding the fork under the table. Mention that for a further test you want him to hold one utensil in each hand. Then you add, "We should have an interval of darkness. Since I can't turn out the restaurant lights, perhaps you could close your eyes."

At this point he holds the spoon in his right hand. He places both hands under the table and takes the fork from you. He holds the fork in his left hand.

Have him place the fork in his jacket pocket. After he's done this, ask him which utensil he holds. He'll say he holds the spoon. Tell him to open his eyes. He'll be amazed to learn that he doesn't hold the spoon. He holds the fork. The spoon and fork have changed places *while* he was holding them.

For the final test you openly and slowly bend the fork so it is obviously curved out of shape. "What happens visibly to the fork happens invisibly to the spoon," you say.

The spectator removes the spoon from his own pocket and finds that it is now bent out of shape!

METHOD: Since the effect can be performed in any restaurant without prior preparation, using utensils that you obviously could not have tampered with previously, the routine smacks of genuine occult powers. But like all such demonstrations, there is a simple answer to the mystery.

A duplicate spoon is used. This may seem to contradict the claim that the trick is impromptu, but there is no contradiction. Restaurants provide not only duplicate spoons, but duplicate forks, knives, glasses and other items of tableware. It is not even necessary to ask for these items since restaurant owners leave them out in the open for easy access.

Perform the trick in a restaurant where you are known. You will, after all, be using their silverware.

As you walk into the restaurant, let your guest go in first. As you pass an empty table, pick up a spoon and slip it into your jacket sleeve. the spectator is ahead of you and doesn't see this.

At the table, when you are seated and waiting for your meal, get the subject of conversation around to the occult. Tell your guest you would like to try a simple experiment in prophecy. On a slip of paper write, "You will choose the spoon." Fold the slip and place it on the table in front of the spectator.

Ask for his fork and spoon. Place them under the table as you explain that you want him to make a completely random choice of one utensil. Leave the fork on your knee. Slip the duplicate spoon out of the jacket sleeve. Hold a spoon in each hand by the bowls so that the handles point toward the spectator. Have him choose one utensil by reaching under the table, taking a utensil and bringing it up into view.

The chosen utensil is the spoon. Have the spectator open the prediction so he can verify that you correctly predicted he would choose the spoon.

As he's reading the prediction, you still have a spoon under the table. Give the handle of the spoon a bend. When the spectator has finished reading the prediction, tell him to reach under the table and grasp the fork by the handle. He is to use the left hand since the visible spoon is in his right hand.

When he grasps the utensil under the table, he thinks he is getting the fork but actually he grasps the duplicate spoon.

Take the visible spoon from him (the one he chose in the first part of this routine) and place it under the table. Tell him to grasp it by the handle, using his right hand. As soon as the spoon is out of sight, switch it for the fork on the knee. The spectator thinks he now holds the spoon in his right hand.

He closes his eyes and places what he thinks is the fork into his jacket pocket. In fact it's the bent spoon. Mutter a magic word, and while his eyes are closed, get rid of the extra spoon by placing it on an adjoining table.

Ask him which utensil he holds in his right hand. He'll say the spoon. Have him open his eyes and bring the utensil up into view. It isn't the spoon. It's the fork. The spoon and fork have changed places while he held them.

You have nothing further to do in terms of method, so build up the occult angle. Take the fork from him and slowly bend it. Remark that the spoon will act in sympathy, and that the spoon will bend by unseen forces while it is in his pocket.

When the fork has been bent, direct the spectator to remove the spoon from his pocket. He does, and discovers that it bent out of shape while it was in his possession.

SLATE SORCERY

Before the invention of parchment, messages were written on stone or wood. Slate was a convenient substance to use because slate writing could be washed off and the slate surface used again for further messages. For centuries mentalists have used slates, both to divine written messages and to cause spirit messages to appear.

Slates are easily obtainable in department and novelty stores. You should use a slate measuring about 9 inches by 12 inches. Choose a soft yellow chalk for maximum visibility.

In this chapter you will learn how to reveal writing, and even pictures, done on the slate. A basic concept called a slate count is described in conjunction with a trick where someone from the spirit world causes a message to appear on a slate. There is also a curiosity where a slate containing a spectator's writing is sent into hyperspace; when the slate returns, the writing has reversed itself.

It is fitting that this chapter opens and closes with routines made available by Robert Parrish. Mr. Parrish is one of the outstanding talents in mentalism and his slate secrets have no peer for ingenuity.

❧ 45. TELLTALE SLATE ❧

A slate and a piece of chalk are given to a spectator. He is asked to write the numbers 1 to 5 in a column along the left side of the slate. When he's done this, he is requested to write the name of his favorite TV show next to any one of the five numbers. The mentalist turns his back while the writing is done.

After the spectator has completed the writing, the slate is handed to someone else. He writes the name of a TV show he never watches next to any available number. At no time does the mentalist see any of the writing.

The slate is passed to each of three other spectators. Each writes down the name of a TV show he never watches. When the writing is complete, the slate will contain a list of five TV shows. One of them is a spectator's favorite, and the other four are not. It is the mentalist's task to figure out which show is the first spectator's favorite.

Without asking a single question, the mentalist goes on to reveal the spectator's favorite TV show. There is no guesswork and there are no gimmicks. The mentalist is right every time he does the trick.

METHOD: This brilliant trick is an invention of Robert Parrish. All that is needed is the slate and a piece of chalk.

Have the first spectator write the name of his favorite TV show anywhere on the slate. Turn your back while he does the writing. When he's finished, have him turn the slate writing-side down. Take the slate from him and pass it on to a second spectator. As you approach the second spectator with the slate, rub the right forefinger along the underside of the slate as shown in Figure 51. This is done secretly, merely as a gesture while you walk over to the second spectator.

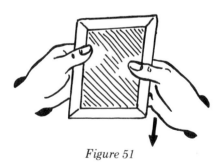

Figure 51

What you have done is cause the name just written to be slightly streaked. This means that you can always tell which name was written on the slate by the first spectator.

The second, third, fourth and fifth spectators each write a name on the slate. When you get the slate, just note which name has the slight streak in the chalk writing. Pretend to be receiving mental impressions. Ask the first spectator a number of questions which seem to have importance ("What kind of car do you drive? What's your favorite sport? Favorite movie?")

As he answers each question, erase one of the names on the slate. Continue erasing names until you are left with just one name, the one with the slight streak in it. Have the spectator reveal to the audience his favorite tv show, then turn the slate around to show that you correctly guessed it.

46. HANDWRITING

Here is another use for the principle suggested by Mr. Parrish. You can, by the use of this method, identify the writing done by each of three different people.

Ask the first spectator to write the numbers 1, 2, 3 in a column on the left side of the slate. Then tell him to write down the name of his favorite car next to any one of the three numbers.

Take the slate from him and give it to the second spectator. As you do, run the right forefinger along the writing side of the slate. This will create a streak or smudge in the first spectator's writing.

Tell the second spectator to write down the name of his favorite car in one of the remaining spaces. After he's done this, take the slate from him and hand it to a third spectator. Of course you must make it obvious that you never see the writing.

As you hand the slate to the third spectator, the right forefinger is again run down the writing side of the slate, but the finger is extended a little farther over.

After the third spectator has jotted down the name of his favorite car, he gives you the slate. In looking over the writing, you will find one name has two streaks or chalk smudges in it. This is the car written by the first spectator.

Another name on the slate has one smudge. This is the car chosen by the second spectator. The name that has no smudge is the car chosen by the third spectator.

This is an excellent mental routine. In handling the slate, you should pretend to study the style used by each writer to jot down his favorite car. Then, pretending that you are getting the impression by handwriting analysis, you proceed to guess which sort of man would choose which car.

47. THOUGHTS IN COLOR

After doing the Parrish trick many times, I developed another method, which allows you to perform it as follows. After the third spectator wrote down the name of his favorite car, he held the slate up. The mentalist, standing fifteen feet away, looks over the names of the cars written on the slate, then tells which car belongs to which spectator. The idea here is that in standing some distance away from the slate, you would have no chance to look closely at the slate to find smudges.

METHOD: Hand out a box of colored chalk. While your back is turned, each of three spectators chooses a piece of chalk. The first spectator writes down the name of his favorite car, then pockets the chalk or returns it to the chalkbox. When he has done this and has turned the slate so the writing side is down, take the slate from him and hand it to a second spectator. Secretly run your forefinger lightly along the underside of the slate as you bring the slate to the second spectator.

Turn your back and have the spectator write the name of his favorite car using a different color chalk. While your back is turned, note the color of the chalk smudge on your right forefinger. This is the color used by the first spectator.

Take the slate from the second spectator. In handing it to the third spectator, run your forefinger lightly along the writing side of the slate. Again it will pick up chalk marks. One color will be the color used by the first spectator, which you already know. The other color is that used by the second spectator.

You now know the color chalk used by each of the first two spectators. The remaining color on the slate will be the color used by the third spectator. Knowing each color, you also know which spectator chose which car. Go on from here with a dramatic revelation.

48. SPIRIT WRITING

It is possible that the earliest tricks done with slates were those in which someone from the spirit world was called upon to write something on a slate. Tricks of this nature have an eerie effect on laymen because it seems that you have established contact with a ghostly presence from another world.

As the audience sees it, you show two slates to be blank. Then you place them together with a small piece of chalk between them. The idea is that you will try to contact a spirit and have him write something with the chalk.

A person in the audience is requested to ask a question about some future wish or dream. The person might ask, "Will I take a trip around the world?"

The mentalist holds the two slates together. As he concentrates, the audience can *hear* the invisible spirit write something on one of the slates. The sound is unmistakable. When the slates are separated, it is seen that a ghostly hand has answered the question with the words, "I think so."

METHOD: The principle behind this routine is an important one in slate work called a slate count. It allows you apparently to show each side of two slates. The audience sees that each side is blank. In fact there is secret writing on one side of one slate, which the audience never sees until the end of the trick.

The prior preparation is this. On one slate write the words, "I think so" in shaky handwriting, using a piece of chalk. If you are right-handed, do the chalk writing with your left hand. If the writing isn't shaky enough, try writing the words upside down. Just make sure the letters are large and clear so that the audience can see exactly what is written. Put the number "1" in the upper-left corner as shown in Figure 52.

Place this slate on the table with the writing side up. Place a second slate on top of it. This completes the preparation.

Figure 52

When you are ready to perform spirit writing, hold the two slates squared in the left hand. You are going to show that each slate surface is blank. Point to the blank face of the uppermost slate, and say, "One." Using the chalk, write the number "1" in the upper-left corner.

Grasp both slates at the upper right corner, Figure 53, and turn them over together, end-over-end, in the direction of the arrow. Place them into the left hand after you've turned them over.

Point to the uppermost blank face and say, "Two." Write the number "2" in the upper-left corner of this slate.

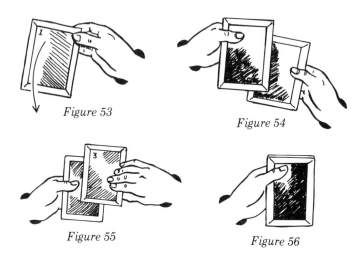

Figure 53

Figure 54

Figure 55

Figure 56

Now take the top slate with the right hand and place it under the other slate as shown in Figure 54. Point to the exposed surface of the top slate and say, "Three." Write a "3" in the upper-left corner.

The handling at this point is important. Grip the top slate with the right hand, fingers on top, thumb below, as shown in Figure 55. Turn the slate over end-for-end and place it on top of the other slate.

The situation now is as shown in Figure 56. Slide the left thumb so that it hides the "1" you wrote earlier. Tip the front of this slate down so that the audience can see the blank surface. Point to it and say, "Four." Then tip the slate up so that only you can see the slate face. Write a "4" in the upper left corner. But note that what you really do is convert the "1" to a "4." This clever idea is based on an Annemann-Hull slate count. It's technical name is a four-as-four count.

The audience thinks they have seen each blank side of two different slates. Drop a small piece of chalk on top of the slates.

Then place the top slate on the table and put the other slate on top of it. The chalk is now between the two slates.

Pick up the two slates and hold them in the hands. Have someone in the audience stand and ask the spirit a question about the future. The question must be of a form where it can logically be answered by "I think so." This answer is general enough to cover many different types of questions, but sometimes you may have to rephrase the question.

As an example, if someone asks, "Should I buy a blue dress or a red dress for the party," you would reword the question as: "The lady would like to know if she should buy a blue dress for the party."

When the question has been asked, the audience will begin to hear a spirit write something on the inside of the two slates. To accomplish this, secretly scratch your fingernail on the underside of the slates. The sound produced is exactly the same as the sound that chalk makes when you write on a slate.

After a moment or two, lift the upper slate and show that the spirit has written an answer to the spectator's question.

49. FACES AND SLATES

Ask four people in the audience to stand. While you jot down their names on a slate, your medium goes into an adjoining room.

Now ask three of the four people to sit down. When this is done there will be one person left standing. Hand the slate to that person and ask him to gaze intently at his own name on the slate.

Then any other person takes the slate to the medium. The medium has no idea which person is standing, yet she erases three of the names on the slate. The name remaining on the slate is the name of the person still standing.

METHOD: The person who brings the slate to the medium doesn't know it, but he (or she) unconsciously codes the proper name to the medium. It is all done instantaneously, quite literally at a glance.

First, in any reasonably large gathering of people, about half will be men. And about half of them will have blue eyes. The rest will have brown eyes.

The other people will be women, some with blue eyes and some with brown eyes. This means that you can choose any one of four different types of person to carry the slate in to the medium: a blue-eyed male, a brown-eyed male, a blue-eyed female or a brown-eyed female. By picking the right person, you code to the medium which of the four names on the slate is the right one.

The test works as follows. Have the medium escorted into another room and the door closed. You can have a committee of one or two people stay with her to insure that all is fair.

Now have four people stand. Write down the first name of each person on a slate, in a column. Remark that you'd like to use the wealthiest person for this test. Have each of the four spectators count how much change he has in his pocket. The person with the most change remains standing. The other three sit down.

Beforehand you and the medium have decided on this code. If a blue-eyed male hands her the slate, the person who remains standing is the first one listed on the slate. If a brown-eyed male hands her the slate, the person is the second name on the slate.

If a blue-eyed female brings her the slate, the person standing is the third name on the slate. If a brown-eyed female brings the slate, then the fourth name on the slate is the correct one.

As soon as the medium is handed the slate she knows, just by glancing at the person who brought the slate, which is the correct name. She erases the three incorrect names and then reveals she knew who is the wealthiest person in the room.

50. IT'S MURDER

If you and the medium know the names of the people who participate in the test, there is an easier method. When circumstances permit, the medium can know the person standing *before* the slate is given to her.

The trick is based on a word code. The idea is to code the correct name to the medium by means of a spoken word which she can hear. But it is not the mentalist who codes the proper word to the medium. This would be too obvious. Instead, the code word is delivered by a spectator.

As before, you have four people stand. The medium glances at them as she leaves the room. Since she knows their names, she simply remembers them in order from left to right. Say the names are Mary, John, Kathie, Diane.

Tell the four spectators that you will enact a murder mystery. They are to pretend that someone has been murdered and one of them is the murderer. Have them decide among themselves who is best qualified as the murderer. That person can be any one of the four. Jot down the names of the four people as they talk among themselves, in the order Mary, John, Kathie, Diane.

If the person designated as the murderer is Mary, hand the slate to any spectator and tell him, "Knock on the door and tell the medium that we're ready." When the medium hears the knock, she knows that the murderer is the first person, Mary. She knows this *because* the spectator knocked on the door to tell the medium that they were ready.

If the murderer is John (the second name on the slate), hand the slate to a spectator and say, "Tell the medium that we're ready." Note that in this case the spectator does not knock on the door. Because of this, the medium knows that the murderer is the second person on the list.

If the murderer is Kathie (third on the list), say to the spectator, "Open the door and hand the medium the slate." Now the medium doesn't hear the spectator say anything and, because of this, knows the murderer is the third person.

In the final case, where the murderer is Diane, turn to a spectator, hand him the slate and say, "Tell her to come out now." Note that the spectator doesn't walk to the door. He simply instructs the medium to join the group. When she comes into view, she takes the slate, pretends to study the face of each spectator, then erases three of the names on the slate. In this case, the medium knows that the murderer is the fourth name on the slate, so she goes on with the revelation from there.

51. HYPERSPACE

Psychics claim the ability to send an object into another dimension. Thus, if a psychic causes a coin to vanish, he says that the coin slipped into the fourth dimension. It is still present, but it is invisible, having entered a higher space.

An important variation on this theme is to send an object into hyperspace *and then bring it back.* One of the strangest examples on this theme is the following routine.

An ordinary slate is placed under the table by the spectator. With the slate resting up against the underside of the tabletop, the spectator writes any word on the slate, Figure 57.

With the slate still under the table, the mentalist takes it and says he will send it into hyperspace and then bring it back. In

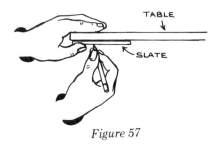

Figure 57

the process, he claims, the writing on the slate will undergo a strange transformation.

After a moment the mentalist says, "It's gone ... Now it's back. Let's see what happened to the writing. What word did you write?"

The spectator might have written the word "them." When the slate is brought into view, it is seen that the writing has indeed changed. It is still the spectator's writing, it is still the word "them," but the word is now the mirror image of itself!

METHOD: All you need are a slate and a piece of chalk. The trick is self-working. Simply follow the presentation given above and the spectator's writing becomes a mirror-image of itself.

There is a follow-up trick you can do with a result that is even more unexpected. Many cars on the road have V-8 engines. Write "V-8" on a piece of paper. Then hand the spectator the slate and chalk.

The spectator places the slate under the table. Using the chalk he writes V-8 on the slate. The writing is done with the slate up against the underside of the tabletop as described above.

Take the slate from the spectator. Still keeping the slate

under the table, tell the spectator that you will slide the slate into hyperspace and then bring it back. Remind him that he wrote the letter "V" first, and then the digit "8."

Rap the slate against the underside of the table, stall for effect, then bring the slate out. The chalk writing has not been altered, but now the "8" is first and the "V" second. The writing thus reads 8-V. The letter and the number, written in the spectator's own handwriting, have changed places!

52. THE ISIS SLATE

While the medium is in another room, the mentalist has someone open a telephone book to any page and note any phone number. Glancing at the name and address of the person whose number was chosen, the mentalist says, "I know the area where this person lives. There are two cross streets. Here's a simple map of the area."

The mentalist draws a map on a slate as shown in Figure 58. "The medium doesn't know these streets," the mentalist says, "But she can project her thoughts to this intersection and visualize the name of the party you picked from the phone book."

The slate and chalk are handed to a spectator to take to the medium. She glances at the map, thinks for a moment, and

Figure 58

then writes four digits on the slate. The four digits are the last four of the chosen phone number.

METHOD: Though this may seem impossible, the two lines drawn on the slate actually code the four-digit telephone number to the medium. The method is bold but certain, and gives the appearance of being genuine telepathy.

Preparation consists of writing, in pencil, the digits 1 through

9, plus 0, along the top of the slate. Then these same digits are repeated along the right edge of the slate, the bottom of the slate, and again on the left side of the slate. The complete preparation appears as shown in Figure 59. Of course in actual practice the pencil writing is invisible on the black slate surface.

When the spectator chooses a phone number, it is natural for you to note it also since you are going to sketch a map of the location of the chosen party. Secretly note the last four digits of the chosen phone number.

Say the digits are 2837. The first digit you code will be from the row of numbers on the top of the slate. The second digit of

Figure 59

Figure 60

the phone number will be coded from the bottom row of numbers on the slate. Simply draw a line connecting these two numbers, as shown in Figure 59.

The third digit of the chosen phone number is coded from the column of digits on the left, and the fourth digit from the column of digits on the right. Simply draw a line connecting the proper digit on the left with the proper digit on the right.

In our example the third and fourth digits of the chosen phone number are 3 and 7. They would be connected together by a line as shown in Figure 60.

Of course you draw the lines casually as you tell the spectator you will draw a map of the area representing the chosen phone number. The two lines look like they might possibly be a street map, so your explanation is logical. Certainly no one ever suspects that two straight lines can be used to code a four-digit telephone number.

Hand the slate and chalk to the spectator. He takes the apparatus to the medium. She pretends to study the map. Actually she notes the digit at the top and the digit at the bottom that are connected together by the first line. Immediately she knows the first two digits of the chosen phone number.

Then she notes the digit at the left and the digit at the right which are connected by a line and she knows the last two digits of the chosen number. All that remains is to turn the slate over and jot down these four digits.

It is true that the medium didn't get the exchange (the first three digits of the phone number), but this point can be covered by having the spectator fill in the first three digits. The medium takes the chalk and immediately fills in the last four digits. It is an amazing demonstration.

53. EPIC SLATE TEST

This is a streamlined version of a classic slate trick. The routine commences as the mentalist hands a spectator a sealed envelope. The envelope contains a four-digit number which will serve as a prediction.

The mentalist explains that he is going to have four numbers, each of four digits, written on the slate. The mentalist will write two of the numbers and volunteers from the audience will write the others. The mentalist will total the numbers and have the total checked. Then it will be determined how closely this total matches the prediction.

To begin, the mentalist has two people think of a year in their lives when something memorable happened. Before they answer, the mentalist writes down two four-digit numbers on the slate.

He shows these two numbers to the audience. Then he asks for the four-digit number thought of by the first spectator. When this number is given, say 1921 is the number, the mentalist writes it down on the slate.

The other spectator mentions his four-digit number. Say it is 1939. This number is also written down on the slate. The mentalist totals up the four numbers. He then hands the slate to another spectator to verify that the addition is correct.

Say the total is 9891. When the prediction envelope is opened and the prediction read, it is found that the prediction stated that the total would be 9891, exactly correct.

METHOD: The slate addition test is generally done with prepared slates or other gimmicks. The present method, devised by Tony Bartolotta and the author, does not use gimmicks. All you need is the slate, the chalk, and the prediction.

The wording of the prediction is, "The total will be 9891." Fold the slip of paper in half and in half again. Seal it in an envelope. If you are performing in a platform or stage show, you can arrange to mail the prediction to the person in charge of the show. Ask him to take the sealed envelope to the show with him.

When ready to perform the routine, explain to the audience that you have a sealed prediction, which is in the hands of someone in the audience. Have that person stand. Then explain that you want each of two people to choose a memorable year in their lives. You further explain that you too will think of two different numbers. But you will try to make you mind receptive to the volunteers so that your thoughts will be influenced by theirs.

On the slate, at the top, write the number 1686. Leave a space, then write 1881. The result thus far is shown in Figure 61.

Turn the slate toward the audience and allow them a brief glance at the writing. Then turn the writing side of the slate back so only you can see it. But in so doing, turn the slate around end-for-end. The result is that the slate will appear as shown in Figure 62. By turning the slate end-for-end, you have converted the first number, 1686, into the predicted total.

Ask the first spectator for his number. Jot it down at the top of the slate. Ask the second spectator for his number and jot it

Figure 61   Figure 62   Figure 63

down under the first number. The slate now looks like Figure 63. Only you can see the writing on the slate.

Explain that you will total the numbers. In fact you know what the total must be, so all you have to do is figure out a fourth number that will give you the desired total of 9891. In our example you would add 1921 + 1939 + 1881 and arrive at 5741. Jot this number down in the lower right corner of the slate and subtract it from the desired total of 9891. The result is 4150. Write 4150 as the fourth number on the slate *as if* you were writing the grand total. With the right thumb erase the figuring you did at the lower right corner. The figuring takes only a few seconds and it appears as if you were simply figuring the grand total. It is important to remember *not* to put commas in the numbers (i.e., 1975, *not* 1,975) or the trick will be revealed when you turn the slate.

After you've jotted down the number 4150 in the space between 1881 and 9891, your work is finished. Remember that your writing will appear to the audience that you are jotting down the grand total.

Hand the slate to another spectator and have him verify the addition. This process will be speeded up if there is a pocket calculator handy. When he has verified the arithmetic, have him erase all numbers except the grand total. Thus the only number on the slate will be 9891. Finally, have the envelope opened and the prediction read aloud. It is seen that you correctly predicted the grand total of the four numbers.

54. PICTURE ESP

If there were a perfect trick, it would be one where the method would fit naturally as part of the effect, and further, if a gimmick were involved, it would dispose of itself. This routine by Robert Parrish is just such a trick, an undisputed masterpiece in the realm of ingenious invention. Not only is the gimmick created before the spectator's eyes but, after it does its work, it literally evaporates into thin air.

Probably the most effective demonstration of mentalism from the standpoint of an audience is the picture duplication test. In this routine, it is built up in dramatic form and makes an excellent climax for a series of mental effects.

A person is invited up to assist. He or she is given a slate and chalk with which to draw any simple geometric design he chooses. When he has completed the drawing, his slate is covered with another slate. This has the effect of sealing his drawing between two slates, making it impossible for anyone to get an accidental glimpse of the design.

The mentalist now picks up another slate, concentrates for a moment, then draws a design on his slate. He holds his slate up. The spectator shows his drawing to the audience. The mentalist shows his drawing to the audience. The drawings are the same!

METHOD: You will need three slates and some chalk. Also needed is a damp cloth to clean off the slates.

Before presenting this routine for the audience, scribble something—numbers, words or pictures—on all three slates. This gives you an excuse to clean the slates later. It seems innocent enough, but it will be used in an ingenious way to achieve the desired end.

Begin by asking a spectator up. Pick up one of the slates. You notice that it has scribbling on it. Take the damp cloth and clean the slate. Then hand it to the spectator. Ask him to think of a simple geometric design and to draw it carefully on the slate.

While he does the drawing with a piece of chalk, turn your back and walk away. Make it obvious that you do not want to see what he is drawing on the slate. Tell the spectator to hold the slate up so that only he can see the drawing.

When he's finished making the drawing, pick up a second slate, clean it off with the damp cloth and step directly in front of the spectator. Say, "I want you to concentrate on your drawing. Don't let anyone see it. We'll cover it with this slate."

This is where the method comes into play. You place the just-cleaned slate on top of his slate as shown in Figure 64. Because your slate is newly washed, its surface acts like a reflecting mir-

Figure 64

ror. So, as you place this slate against his, the slate gives you a perfect reflection of his drawing.

Tell the spectator to hold the two slates together. You then step back to the table and pick up the third slate. Wash it off with the cloth. Pretend to concentrate. Draw something on the slate. Shake your head, tell the spectator you're not getting a clear impression, and erase your drawing.

Concentrate another thirty seconds. Then draw a duplicate of the design you saw in the reflection of his slate. Take your time doing this. The trick is over as far as you're concerned, but the audience thinks that you are attempting the impossible problem of duplicating a thought-of-picture and assumes it will take a good deal of time to get the spectator's thought.

When you've completed your drawing, hold you slate up over your head, but with the drawing side away from the audience.

Tell the spectator to show the audience what he has drawn on his slate. Immediately turn your slate around to show that you duplicated his design. The trick seems impossible and will bring a strong round of applause.

Note that when you washed the chalk off a second slate, the slate acted like a reflecting mirror, but that after a few moments the moisture evaporated. This left the spectator with two ordinary slates and not a clue as to how the effect was achieved.

MIRACLES WITH CARDS

The best mental effects with cards are those which avoid the appearance of card trickery while emphasizing the paranormal aspect of the demonstration. Such effects are always greeted as experiments in mind reading and will be enthusiastically received by your audience. This chapter offers a collection of some of the best mind-reading tricks with cards.

55. SLEIGHT OF MIND

Mind reading and gambling always attract wide interest. The following routine combines both subjects in a stunning demonstration of telepathic ability.

Using a borrowed, shuffled deck, the mentalist deals out poker hands to each of five players. But this is no ordinary game of poker. He asks each player to mix his cards, and to think of any card in his poker hand.

The poker hands are gathered and placed on top of the deck. The mentalist states that while gamblers need sleight of hand and years of practice to control the cards, those with psychic ability can control the cards with sleight of mind.

The mentalist deals out five poker hands from the top of the deck. He asks the first player to indicate which poker hand contains his chosen card. The mentalist picks up the indicated poker hand, studies the cards, and immediately names the thought-of card.

Exactly this same procedure is followed with each of the other players. The mentalist asks no questions and does not know the thought-of cards until he picks up a poker hand. But despite the impossibility of what he is attempting to do, the mentalist succeeds every time in revealing the thought-of cards.

METHOD: Using any borrowed, well-shuffled deck, deal out five hands of five cards each. The deal is the standard dealing procedure for draw poker. You deal from left to right, giving a card to each player on each round. When you've dealt out the five hands, ask each person to pick up his poker hand, mix the cards, think of one card in his hand and mix the cards again. Clearly you could not possibly know the identity of the thought-of cards.

Take the fifth person's hand and put it on top of the deck. Continue to gather the poker hands from right to left by placing the fourth person's hand on top of the deck, then the third hand, then the second and then the first.

Talk about psychic powers, about how sleight of hand can be replaced by sleight of mind. Now deal out five poker hands again, dealing from left to right, a card at a time to each player, until each poker hand has five cards.

Pick up the first hand. Be careful not to disturb the cards. They must remain in the order you dealt them. Fan the cards and ask the first spectator if he sees his card in this poker hand. If he doesn't, put this poker hand down, pick up the second poker hand and fan these cards. Ask the first spectator if he sees his card in this hand.

If he doesn't see his card in the second hand, put the second hand down. Pick up the third hand, then the fourth and, if necessary, the fifth, until he says that he does see his card.

The key to the working is remarkably simple. No matter which hand contains the *first* spectator's card, the thought-of card will be the *first* card in that poker hand. By first card we mean the first card dealt to that hand, the face card or bottom card of the poker hand.

After you reveal the first spectator's card, turn attention to the second spectator. Show him each poker hand in turn until he says that he sees his card. The *second* spectator's card will be the *second* card in the poker hand.

Similarly, the third person's card will be the third card in its hand; the fourth person's card will be the fourth in its hand; and the fifth person's card will be the fifth card in its hand. Each spectator must tell you which hand contains his card. One poker hand may contain more than one of the thought-of cards. But the rule is always the same. Once you have been told which hand contains a thought-of card, you directly name that card.

This completes the routine. To vary the revelation, when you know which hand contains the third spectator's card, and which hand contains the fourth spectator's card, don't reveal the thought-of cards. Just remark that you will come back to these hands later.

After you have revealed the first, second and fifth chosen cards, return to the cards you haven't revealed. Pick up the hand containing the third spectator's card. With the poker hand face-down, perform an Under/Down shuffle by dealing the top card under the packet, the next card down onto the table, the next card under the packet, the next card down, and so on until you have one card left. This card will be the third spectator's thought-of card.

Now pick up the packet containing the fourth spectator's card. This packet must be a different one from the packet containing the third spectator's card. Perform a Down/Under shuffle with the poker hand containing the fourth spectator's card. Here you deal the first card down onto the table. The next card is placed under the packet. The next card is dealt down onto the table, the next dealt under the packet and so on until you have one card left. This card will be the fourth spectator's thought-of card.

This procedure for handling the revelation of the third and fourth cards is not strictly necessary but if offers a change of pace and deepens the mystery.

56. REMOTE VIEWING

While you stand across the room, a spectator chooses a card from his own shuffled deck, a deck you've never seen before. A second spectator also chooses a card from the same deck. You have no idea what the chosen cards are and they are buried in the center of the deck.

The second spectator cuts the deck and completes the cut. Then he hands the cards to you. This is the first time you have touched the deck. Without asking a question, you run through the deck and find both of the selected cards.

METHOD: While a borrowed deck is being shuffled and cut, explain that it's possible for the mind to leave the body and focus on a remote event.

To demonstrate how this works, you will project an invisible focal point behind the spectator, so that you can, in effect, look over his shoulder as he mentally chooses a card.

You now walk to a distant corner of the room and face the spectator. Have him cut off about half the deck, turn it face-up and drop it on top of the balance of the deck. When he does this he will have a face-up portion of cards back to back with a face-down portion.

Tell him to spread the cards until he comes to the last face-up card. He holds the cards up so that only he can see the face-up cards. He spreads the deck until he reaches the face-up card nearest the center of the deck. In Figure 65, the spectator's view, he would note the Four of Diamonds.

The important point is *your* view of the situation. The spectator holds the deck up between the hands. You are across the room. From your view the situation is as shown in Figure 66. All you need do is note the bottom card of the deck. In Figure 66 it is the Two of Diamonds.

Once the spectator has noted his card, tell him to square up the deck. Have him hand the deck to someone else. This person turns the deck over, spreads the cards and notes the face-up

Figure 65   *Figure 66*

card that is now the last face-up card, that is, the face-up card nearest to the face-down portion at the middle of the deck.

Since he has turned the deck over to look at his card, there is a new card facing you at the bottom of the deck. This card may be the Ace of Spades. All you need to remember are the Two of Hearts and the Ace of Spades. From your point of view the trick is over.

Tell the spectator to square up the deck. Then have him lift off all of the face-up cards, turn them over and place them down on top of the face-down portion. After he has done this, the entire deck will be face-down. Tell him to cut the deck and complete the cut.

He hands the deck to you. Spread the deck between the hands, from left to right, with the faces of the cards toward you. Look for your two key cards, the Two of Diamonds and the Ace of Spades. The first person's card will be directly to the right of the Two of Diamonds. The second person's card will be directly to the right of the Ace of Spades.

Following the presentation given earlier, pretend you have received a mental picture of the selected cards by means of remote viewing. The strength of the trick derives from the fact that you do not handle the deck until the very end of the routine.

♦ 57. EVEN-MONEY PROPOSITION

It is believed that at some early point in history human beings had the ability to distinguish colors by sense of touch alone. In some tests it appears that some people have a limited ability to distinguish light colors from dark by touch.

Using ordinary playing cards one can test whether a person has the gift of distinguishing colors by the sense of touch. The person will be asked to guess if a card is red or black. In this demonstration, the person will always be right.

The volunteer is not influenced in any way, he can change his mind, yet he always makes the correct choice. Since the spectator does all the guessing, there is no way to fake the outcome.

METHOD: Arrange 13 cards as follows from the top down: R-B-B-R-R-B-B-R-R-B-B-R-R. Note that a basic R-B-B-R stack appears three times with an extra red card at the bottom of the stack. This stack of 13 cards is placed on top of the deck until you are ready to perform.

To present this routine, get the discussion around to the subject of sensing color by touch. Many experiments here and in Europe hint at the existence of such abilities. The easiest test, you explain, is one where a volunteer is asked to distinguish, by sense of touch alone, a dark color from a light color.

As you talk, pick up the deck and place it in your left hand. The left thumb pushes over cards one at a time to the right.

Don't reverse the order of the cards or otherwise disturb the stack. Push over the top 13 cards, and take this packet with your right hand. Place it on the table, face-down.

Now turn the deck face-up and remove one red card and one black card. Place them face-up on the table, about twelve inches from one another. Explain that these will act as indicator cards. If the spectator thinks that a particular card is red, you will place it on the red indicator. If he guesses that the card is black, you will place it on the black indicator.

Now pick up the 13-card packet and place it face-down in the left hand. Your left thumb pushes the top two cards to the right. Take this pair of cards with your right hand. Turn the right hand over so that the faces of the two cards can be seen. Point out that one card is red and the other is black.

Place this pair of cards on the bottom of the packet. Repeat this same procedure with the next five pairs of cards. Show each pair to consist of one red and one black card, then place the pair of cards on the bottom of the packet. At no time do you disturb or alter the order of the cards in any pair. Treat each pair as a unit.

Tell the spectator that you will use six pairs of cards. After you have shown six pairs, drop the 13-card packet back on top of the deck. Pick off the top two cards. Place them face-down in front of the spectator.

He is allowed to touch each card but he can't look at the face of either card. Ask him to guess, by sense of touch alone, which of the two cards is red. He thinks one card is red and the other black, but of course that is no longer true. Both cards are red, so it makes no difference which card he chooses.

When he has chosen one card, place it face-down on the red indicator card, Figure 67. Put the other card of the pair aside face-down in a discard pile.

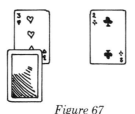

Figure 67

Repeat the procedure for the next pair. Ask the spectator to guess which of these two cards is black. When he makes his guess, place that card face-down on top of the black indicator card. Put the other card of the pair aside face-down in the discard pile.

Repeat the procedure for the next pair. The spectator guesses which of these two cards is red. With the next pair the spectator guesses which card is black. With the fifth pair he guesses which is red, and with the final pair he guesses which is black.

Pick up the discards, casually show the faces, and place this packet on top of the deck. Then stall to build up the climax of the trick. Ask the spectator if he positively had no idea which card was which. He will say no. Ask him if he accidently glimpsed the face of any card. He will say no. Act as if the outcome of the test is in doubt. Remind him that on the average, people get about half the cards right.

Turn up the cards on the red indicator. Turn them up one at a time. When it is seen that the spectator got every one right, say, "Remarkable. This is the first time that's happened!"

Then turn up the cards on the black indicator. The spectator was 100 percent right on every card. Recovering from your astonishment, congratulate him on his extraordinary ability.

58. ULTIMATE MATCH

With a deck of cards in his own hands, a spectator cuts a portion onto the table, looks at the next card, places this card onto the tabled portion, then puts the balance of the deck on top. He alone handles this deck.

Another deck is removed from its case and placed alongside the spectator's deck. At the mentalist's request the spectator takes the top card from each deck, turns each card face-up, and places each in front of its own deck.

This process of dealing cards from the top of each deck continues. Of course the card dealt from the top of the spectator's deck is different from the corresponding card dealt from the top of the other deck.

When the spectator gets to the card he chose, however, an odd thing happens. He turns up the same card from the other deck!

He can continue dealing simultaneously from the tops of both decks but he should turn up no other cards that are an exact match. The only perfect match that is produced is the one with his selected card.

METHOD: The principle behind this trick is associated with Eddie Joseph. Two ordinary decks are used. They should have contrasting back patterns, or back patterns of contrasting color. Say that one deck is blue-backed and the other deck red-backed. Preparation is as follows.

Shuffle the blue-backed deck thoroughly. Then note the top card of this deck. Say it is the Five of Spades. Find the Five of Spades in the red-backed deck and place it on the face (bottom) of the red-backed deck.

Now note the second card from the top of the blue-backed deck. It may be the Three of Diamonds. Find the Three of Diamonds in the red-backed deck and place it second from the face (bottom) of the red-backed deck.

Continue stacking the red-backed deck so that each card from face to top is the same as the cards from top to face of the blue-backed deck. In other words, the setup of the red-backed deck is exactly the reverse of the setup of the blue-backed deck. The bottom card of the red-backed deck is the same as the top card of the blue-backed deck. The card second from the bottom of the red-backed deck is the same as the card second from the top of the blue-backed deck. The card third from the bottom of the red-backed deck is the same as the card third from the top of the blue-backed deck, and so on. The top card of the red-backed deck will be the same as the bottom card of the blue-backed deck. This is called a mirror stack or a reflected stack because one deck is set up as the mirror image of the other deck.

When the decks have been arranged so that one is stacked the reverse of the other, place each deck in its own card case. Whenever the occasion demands, you have simply to toss out the two decks and proceed with a miraculous coincidence trick.

In presenting the trick, explain that you have previously placed a certain card at a certain position in the red-backed deck. This card was chosen so as to coincide with a card that the spectator hasn't selected yet.

Have the spectator remove the blue-backed deck from its case and hold it in his hand. Tell him to cut a packet from the top and place this packet on the table. When he has done this, he looks at the top card of the portion still in his hand. He then places this card on top of the tabled packet. Then he places the portion in his hand on top of his card. The selected card is now buried in the deck somewhere. No one knows its location and only the spectator knows its identity.

Tell the spectator to remove the red-backed deck from its case. He puts the two decks alongside one another face-down. Then he deals cards face-up simultaneously from the tops of both decks. The dealt cards are placed face-up in front of their respective decks.

He continues dealing this way. Point out each time that the card he deals from the blue-backed deck does not match the card from the red-backed deck. The two cards may have the same suit or the same value, but that is a minor coincidence.

The spectator continues dealing until he turns up his card from the blue-backed deck. He will be staggered to discover that he has turned up exactly the same card from the red-backed deck.

59. DOUBLE STOP

This amazing trick, the invention of Frank Taylor, combines two different effects to produce a double-barreled mystery. Two spectators participate. Each person gets about half the deck and chooses a card in a fair manner.

After the cards are replaced in their respective halves of the deck, the spectators commence dealing cards off the top of each packet. At some point the mentalist calls stop.

The card stopped at in one half of the deck is the card chosen by one of the spectators. This in itself is impressive because the mentalist never touched this half of the deck. But there is more.

The other spectator looks at the card stopped at in his half of the deck. It is his selected card. Then the mentalist, without touching the deck, proceeds to reveal the identity of this spectator's card.

METHOD: The routine uses a simple setup and ingenious reasoning to arrive at the double effect. The setup is this. Have 20 red cards on top of the deck, followed by 26 blacks, then the remaining 6 reds on the bottom of the deck.

Follow the handling with the deck in hand and all will be clear. Begin by having spectator A cut off about eight or ten cards from the top of the deck. He places this packet to the left.

Then have him cut about three-quarters of the remainder of the deck, leaving 8 or 10 cards on the table, Figure 68. The large packet is retained by spectator A. On the table are two small

Figure 68

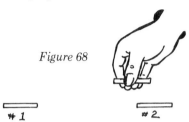

packets of about ten cards each. In Figure 68 they are labeled #1 and #2.

Since spectator A holds the center portion of the deck, there is no way anyone could know the top or bottom card of this packet. Instruct him to look at the top card of his packet. When he has done this, ask him to cut the packet and complete the cut.

You now turn to a second spectator B. Ask him to pick up the packet that was originally on the bottom of the deck. This is packet #2 in Figure 68. He is to shuffle this packet until he is satisfied that it is well mixed.

When he has done this, ask him to note the top card of his packet. Point out that he alone knows the identity of his selected card. When he has noted the top card, ask him to place the packet on the table. He then picks up the other small packet, #1 in Figure 68, shuffles it and drops it on top of his packet.

Remind B that you have not touched his cards thus far, and that you will not touch them *at any time*. This is one of the most baffling features of the trick and one that will bother the most astute observer.

Now turn to spectator A and have him think of his card. Take his packet. Hold it in the left hand. With the faces of the cards toward you, spread the cards between your hands from left to right.

The first group of cards at the face of the packet will be

black. Cut these black cards to the back (top) of the packet. You now have a group of red cards at the face of the packet.

Beginning with the face card, mentally count 20 cards as you push the cards from your left hand to the right. Cut this 20-card group to the back (top) of the packet.

The block of red cards is now in the appropriate center of the packet. If the cards are spread from left to right, the rightmost red card would be 20th from the top of the packet.

You have to do one more thing. Beginning at the top of the packet, mentally count to the first red card. This card will be spectator A's card. Remember the card and its position from the top of the packet. Say the card is the Ten of Hearts and that it is 12th from the top of the packet.

All of the above handling takes only a few seconds to accomplish. As you gain familiarity with the trick you will find that the handling can be done casually and quickly.

Hand the packet back to spectator A. Now ask each person to deal cards from the top of his packet, one at a time, face-down onto the table. You call a stop when spectator A's card is about to be dealt. In our example, this would be when the spectators are about to deal the 12th card from their respective halves of the deck.

The 12th card in B's packet is his card. Ask him to name his card, then have him turn the 12th card face-up. You have stopped him on his thought-of card and you never touched his packet.

Ask spectator A to look at the card you stopped him at. It is his card. Thus you have caused both selected cards to show up at exactly the same time.

For the clincher, ask spectator A to concentrate on his card. He does, and you then go on to reveal the name of his card. In our example it would be the Ten of Hearts. You have performed an extraordinary mystery.

CONFEDERATES

The confederate is someone who pretends to be a spectator in the audience but is in fact an assistant to the mentalist. Properly used, the confederate can be the mentalist's most valued ally in the performance of mental miracles.

A confederate must be used in such a way that he is never suspected. The tricks in this chapter are among the best on the subject. Practice them with the person who will serve as your confederate, making sure that he knows his part well, and you will have on hand an arsenal of tricks that will baffle any audience.

60. FINGER, FINGER

This is one of the most thought-provoking secrets to be evolved in many years. The basic idea seems to have originated in Continental Europe. The present handling was suggested by Bruce Elliott and L. Vosburgh Lyons.

The mentalist turns his back on two spectators who attempt to act as thought transmitters. Both of these spectators hold out from 1 to 5 fingers. The total of the two hands is taken and called aloud. Immediately the mentalist correctly reveals the number of fingers *each* spectator is showing.

The trick is repeated. The spectators stand back to back and hold up from 1 to 5 fingers. Neither spectator can see how many fingers the other holds up. Another person calls out the total. Immediately the mentalist tells how many fingers each spectator is showing.

The conditions can be made even tighter. Each spectator and the mentalist can be blindfolded. Each of the two blindfolded spectators holds up from 1 to 5 fingers. *Any other spectator* calls out the total. The blindfolded mentalist is still correct.

The trick can be repeated several times. Each time the total is different. Each time neither spectator talks, nor does the mentalist speak. Yet each time the mentalist correctly reveals how many fingers each spectator is showing.

METHOD: You already know that one person is a confederate. This is a good point to emphasize that, like all tricks in this chapter, the use of a confederate in "Finger, Finger" is so well concealed that, even knowing there is a confederate, you would be unlikely to guess exactly how the confederate is employed. Thus, even if a sharp spectator suspects a confederate, he cannot see how this would have the slightest bearing on the trick.

The two spectators stand facing one another. One of them is your confederate. By prior agreement between you, the first time the trick is worked, the confederate shows 2 fingers. When the total is called aloud, you mentally deduct 2 from the total. You now know how many fingers the other spectator was showing. If, for example, the total is 6, you know that the confederate held up 2 fingers, so the other spectator must be showing 4 fingers.

For the repeat, the confederate always holds out the same number of fingers as the other spectator did on the previous trial. In our example, when you do the trick the second time, the confederate holds out 4 fingers. The other spectator holds out any number, say 3. When the total is announced, in this case 7, you mentally deduct or subtract 4 from 7 and you know that the other spectator held up 3 fingers.

You can see that it does not matter if the spectators stand facing one another or stand back to back. It does not matter if they are blindfolded or if you are blindfolded. Finally, it does not matter who calls out the total. Thus, all of these seemingly strict conditions are seen to be so much window dressing meant to impress the spectator. In terms of the method, they mean nothing.

When you and the confederate become expert at this mystery, you can try a variation. Whatever number of fingers the spectator holds out on any trial, the confederate holds out one more finger the next time. If the spectator holds out 3 fingers on one trial, the confederate would hold out 4 fingers on the following trial. If the spectator holds out 5 fingers on a trial, the confederate holds out 1 finger on the next trial.

61. COVENANT

The mentalist removes an Ace, Two and Three from the deck. He hands these three cards to a spectator, tells him to place the cards behind his back, mix them, and choose one. When he's done this, he gives the remaining two cards to another spectator.

This party takes the two cards behind his back, mixes them and chooses one. He then hands the remaining card to the third spectator.

All of the mixing and choosing of cards takes place while the mentalist turns his back. He can be blindfolded or out of the room. When each person has a card, the mentalist faces the three people and asks each to concentrate on his card.

Without asking a question, without codes or prompting, the mentalist proceeds to name the card held by each spectator.

METHOD: Of the three spectators, the second or middle spectator is the confederate. Before doing the trick, give the confederate the Two of Hearts and the Three of Clubs. He places these cards in his left jacket sleeve. If he wears a watch, he can tuck them under the watchband so they stay in place. He must remember which card is the Two and which is the Three.

When ready to present the trick, make sure the confederate is standing between the other two spectators. Tell them you would like to try an experiment in mindreading and that you will use an Ace, a Two and a Three.

Spread the deck between your hands, with the faces of the cards toward you. Pretend to remove an Ace, Two and Three. In fact remove three Aces.

Without showing the faces of the three cards, hand them to the first spectator. Tell him to place them behind his back and mix them. Turn your back and walk to a distant corner of the room.

Keeping your back turned, ask the first spectator to take one of the cards without looking at the face, and hand the other two cards to the next spectator. This spectator is your confederate. He takes the two cards behind his back. Tell him to mix them and choose one. But what he does is this. He places the two cards into his right jacket sleeve. Then he removes the Two and the Three from his left sleeve.

He knows which card is the Three, so he keeps this card and gives the Two to the remaining spectator. It appears as if you could not possibly know which spectator holds which card, but you know that the first spectator must have taken an Ace (he had no choice), the second spectator a Three and the last spectator a Two.

Reveal each of the cards in an impressive way. Note that although you do not know the suit of the first card, you know positively it is an Ace. When revealing this card, say, "I can clearly see that it's an Ace, but that's all I'm getting tele-pathically."

Turn to the second spectator and say, "Your card is clearer in my mind. It is a Three. I don't know the suit, but I can see that it's a black Three."

With the third spectator say, "You seem to be sending out the strongest thought wave. Your card is red, a Heart, yes, the Two of Hearts."

62. NAMES IN THE NEWS

A newspaper is given to a spectator. He is asked to take it to a far corner of the room, open it to any page that contains a picture and concentrate on the most prominent person in that picture. If there are two or more celebrities or world leaders in the picture, he is to mentally decide on the one who seems to have the strongest appeal.

No questions are asked. The person opens the newspaper to any page. No one knows the page number. The spectator with the newspaper can even be out of the room. He must concentrate on a picture that is actually in the newspaper, but otherwise there are absolutely no restrictions.

The mentalist writes something on a piece of paper, folds it and places it in a drinking glass. The folded paper is in full view from start to finish.

Now the newspaper is handed to a second spectator. He follows the same procedure. Taking the newspaper to a far corner or into another room, he opens it to any page containing a picture and concentrates on the prominent personality in that picture. The only stipulation is that he must choose a picture that is different from the first person's picture.

The mentalist picks up a second blank sheet of paper. In bold letters he writes something on the paper, folds it and places it into the glass.

Each spectator reveals the name of the person he chose. The two folded pieces of paper are removed from the glass, unfolded and read aloud. It is found that the mentalist correctly perceived which pictures would be chosen.

METHOD: You know that a confederate is used and you may suspect that he sends you some sort of a code, but in fact there is no code. The principle used here is known as the one-ahead principle. It is an important secret in mental work.

With a newspaper handy, you and the confederate decide which picture he is to choose. The choice should be governed by the fact that the picture should be a prominent one, preferably of a celebrity of worldwide fame. In other words, deliberately choose a picture that the spectator himself would be likely to choose. Let us assume here that the picture is one of the President.

The test is performed in a roomful of people. Ask for a volunteer for a test in picture projection. Your confederate should not appear too eager. Let someone else volunteer. Only then does the confederate offer his services. Thus, if it becomes necessary to use a second spectator later on, it will be natural to remember that the confederate also volunteered.

Hand the newspaper to the volunteer spectator. Instruct him to go to a far corner, open the newspaper, leaf though the pages, and finally decide on a page that contains a picture of a prominent personality.

When the spectator tells you he has chosen a photo, ask him to concentrate on it. Then on a large blank sheet of paper write the President's name. Fold the paper and place it into a drinking glass.

Have him tell the others in the room the person he chose. If he chose the President, stop right here. You've performed a miracle. Simply let someone open the paper and verify that you correctly read the spectator's mind.

If the spectator chose another picture, you proceed as if all is going fine. Let's say he chose a picture of a sports figure. You remark, "I'd like someone else to choose a name in the news. Please choose a completely different picture."

Take the newspaper from the first spectator. Glance at the confederate and say, "You volunteered before. Here, you take the newspaper." The confederate takes the paper to a far corner and opens it to the picture of the President.

Pick up another sheet of paper. On this sheet you pretend to write the confederate's thoughts. Actually you write down the name of the sport's figure, fold the paper and place it in the glass.

Have the confederate reveal the name he was concentrating on. Then remove the two pieces of paper from the glass. Toss them out onto the table, mixing the papers up so that no one knows which was the first one you wrote on.

Have each sheet unfolded and read. You correctly got both of the mentally projected pictures.

63. THE FARADAY CAGE

When psychics are tested in laboratories, they are sometimes placed in a special room known as a Faraday Cage. The cage consists of a metal network which blocks out radio signals, guaranteeing that the psychic is not using a confederate who transmits signals to him over a radio transmitter.

When at the home of a friend it is possible to demonstrate a simple variation of the Faraday Cage. There is no special apparatus. You will use a borrowed bag and your host's telephone. The bag acts as a cage. Of course it cannot block out radio waves, but it can be used to block out sound waves.

With everyone watching, you call the operator and ask her to ring the number back. Explain that you've been having trouble adjusting the loudness of the ring and ask that she ring the phone about ten times.

The receiver is replaced on the hook. After a few seconds, the operator begins ringing the number. The ring is loudly heard. You then lower the paper bag over the phone. When the phone is completely covered, the ringing stops. It does not become muffled or faint; it stops completely.

When the paper bag is lifted, the ringing can be heard again. There is nothing ambiguous about the source of the sound. It is coming from the phone. The bag is lowered over the phone.

Immediately the ringing sound stops. When the bag is lifted, the ringing sound is heard again.

You then pick up the phone, thank the operator for her cooperation, and proceed with further mysteries.

METHOD: The secret is simple, but it should be practiced to get the timing correct. In brief, the confederate is at another phone. He dials the number you are at, lets the phone ring, hangs up, dials again, hangs up and dials once more. It is that easy, but proper acting and correct timing are needed to make the illusion perfect.

First, you and the confederate synchronize your watches. Decide between you that when you are at a party that night, you will perform this trick at exactly 10:15.

At 10:14 borrow a paper bag. The bag should be large enough to fit over the telephone. At 10:15 pretend to dial the operator. Actually you pick up the phone, dial 9, then pretend to talk to the operator. Request that she call you back and ask that she allow the phone to ring about ten times so you can adjust the loudness of the bell.

At exactly 10:15 your confederate calls the number you are at. He should get a busy signal because at exactly that time you are pretending to be speaking with the operator. If he gets a busy signal, this insures that you and your confederate are working in synchronization.

Replace the phone on the receiver. Your confederate redials your number. As soon as your phone begins to ring, pick up the paper bag and lower it over the phone. Do this slowly. You want the bag to completely cover the phone after exactly three rings.

At his end of the line, the confederate lets the phone ring three times. Then he breaks the connection and *immediately* redials the number.

From the point of view of the people at the party, they have just seen (or rather, heard) you demonstrate how the ringing sound of the phone can be silenced merely by placing a paper bag over it.

From your point of view, you must mentally keep track of the passing seconds. It takes about ten seconds to dial a number and about three more for the call to go through. Thus, you stall for about 13 seconds, then *slowly* lift the bag up.

The ringing sound of the phone will be heard again as the bag is lifted. This time the confederate allows the phone to ring four times. He then breaks the connection and redials the number.

At your end of the line you allow the phone to ring four times, lower the bag over the phone and demonstrate that once again the phone is completely silent.

Mentally count to 13, then slowly begin to lift the bag. The ringing can be heard again. Pick up the phone, thank the operator (really the confederate) and hang up. You have just completed a memorable experiment in which you demonstrated your control over sound waves.

Practice the trick to get the timing down perfect and you will have a perfect illusion. The one thing that might happen to delay the working is that after the confederate redials the number, it may take four or five seconds for the call to go through. This is acceptable because you slowly and deliberately lift the bag a fraction of an inch at a time. The audience is not exactly sure when they are supposed to hear the ringing sound, so the slight delay will go unnoticed.

The key to the strength of tricks like this one is that you take an everyday object like a telephone and cause it to act in a decidedly uncommon manner. Spectators may suspect complex electronic gimmicks, but all objects are ordinary and there is nothing to find.

64. THE DARKROOM SÉANCE

For this spooky excursion into the paranormal, the mentalist displays an ordinary matchbox. He claims that a ghost lives inside the matchbox and that it is possible to establish communication with the ghost if conditions are right.

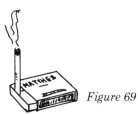

Figure 69

A lit cigarette is wedged upright in the matchbox as shown in Figure 69. Then the lights are turned out in the room. The glowing end of the cigarette can be plainly seen in the darkness by all those sitting at the table.

Any spectator is asked to name the smallest digit in his telephone number. Say he names 3. While everyone watches, the glowing end of the cigarette flares brighter, subsides, flares again, subsides, then flares a third time. The ghost inside the matchbox correctly communicated the chosen digit.

Remarking that one flare will signify yes and two flares no, the mentalist has someone at the table ask the unseen ghost a question. When the question has been asked, the cigarette either flares up once or twice, giving the correct answer to the spectator's question.

At the finish, the lights are turned on. The cigarette and the matchbox can then be passed around for examination.

METHOD: This miniature version of the spirit séance is the clever invention of George Schindler. The confederate is one of the people seated at the table. There is no hookup to the cigarette. To make it flare up, the confederate breathes on the lit end of the cigarette. In the darkened room this is not seen. The illusion created is that the ghost inside the matchbox has taken a puff on the cigarette and thereby caused the lit end to become brighter.

The effect of this miniature darkroom séance is all out of proportion to the simple method and will be remembered for a long time afterwards.

PSYCHOMETRY

This trick, to my mind, is one of the greatest one-man psychic effects used to puzzle an audience. It has all of the elements necessary to make a great talk-maker, and a performer with only a bit of showmanship can't help but make a good thing of it. One with a decent amount of that valuable asset will create an astounding impression whenever he presents this test.

Last, but far from least, the effect needs very little preparation, and it can succeed under most exact conditions. In short, we have before us an idea with unlimited scope.

This is another of those rare secrets wherein the method is nothing and the effect as seen through the eyes of the audience everything. The people who witness the performance of these individual tests will never tumble to the simple detail that makes it possible. The enormity of what the performer attempts completely overshadows the means by which it is accomplished.

The above remarks are taken from the opening paragraphs of "Pseudo Psychometry," an Annemann routine that has become a classic in the field of mentalism. Psychometry is the ability to examine an object like a pen or a ring and immediately identify its owner. Annemann took this simple premise and built it into a routine of stunning magnitude.

Over the years a number of talented mentalists have added to and expanded on the Annemann premise. This, the final chapter, will deal exclusively with psychometry routines. The material given here is among the most important you can learn because it opens the door to cold readings, to identifying people by a handwritten word, to revealing their dates of birth, and even to divining the amount of change they have in their pockets.

65. Pseudo Psychometry

This is the original Annemann article on psychometry. A packet of letter envelopes is all that is needed at any time by the performer. Having left the platform to pass out about a dozen of them to spectators, the performer returns to the front.

Requesting that those with envelopes pay strict attention, the performer continues. They are to put into their envelopes some single article, a personal belonging that they happen to have with them. It can be a fountain pen, tie clasp, ribbon, coin, knife, pencil, handkerchief, ring, in fact *anything* of that nature that can be sealed inside the envelope.

During this time the performer may be turned around so that he in no way sees what is placed into any envelope. This seems important to the audience but it actually means nothing insofar as the working of the trick goes.

Once the envelopes are ready, the performer has them collected by a member of the audience and brought forward. This spectator mixes them and hands one to the performer. He tears off the end of the envelope and dumps the contents into his hand. Turning whatever object it might be over and over, he describes a person, giving a description of that person's appearance, attire and approximate age. He then holds the article for all to see and asks the owner to acknowledge it. The person stands. He is exactly the one described by the mentalist!

Another envelope is opened and the article once more seemingly gives a clue regarding the characteristics of the owner. This time, however, the performer walks among the audience and suddenly returns the article *directly to its owner!*

As each envelope is handed him, the performer successfully describes the owner or locates the owner in the audience. The patter is about psychometry. Mediums of this type have the ability to "see" and locate people by touching some personal belonging. In this case, instead of revealing information that may be of a confidential nature, the performer is able, through the same power, to describe and locate the owner of the article he handles.

METHOD: The members of the audience never realize that the important detail is right under their noses. They all try to fathom how the performer is able to trace the owner of the trinket each time, it being obvious that he didn't see what any person furnished or know in what order the mixed envelopes might be collected and given to him.

As you will see, the test can be made large or small, fast or slow, as desired.

The secret lies entirely in the envelopes. It is only necessary to know to whom each envelope belongs. Annemann's method of marking is to open an envelope with the flap toward the performer, and write a figure lightly on the inside of the envelop about an inch from one end. Number all the envelopes and have them in order from 1 to 10.

It is far from difficult to remember who gets these envelopes as they are passed out in numerical order from left to right; by skipping a person (or by using people in aisle seats) the envelopes are spread through the crowd in an order the performer can trace.

After each spectator has sealed an object in his or her envelope, have the envelopes collected and mixed. When one is handed to you, tear it open with the flap toward you. Tear off a half-inch from the left-hand end. Your right thumb and fingers are at the top and bottom edges with the flap now turned toward the floor. The contents are tipped into the left hand. The number is near the edge of the inside, looking at you, as in Figure 70. If the number is 7, you know the contents of this envelope belong to the 7th spectator.

Figure 70

Glance in his or her direction to get the physical description of the person. Then pretend to receive a mental impression from studying the article you just tipped out of the envelope.

You can describe the owner of the article or you can leave the stage and return the article to the person directly. Build up this part of the trick because it is inherently dramatic.

Dog-ear one envelope instead of marking it inside. When you get to it you know the owner without opening the envelope. You apparently get a stronger impression this time. Describe the person, locate him and return the envelope still sealed.

A marvelous stage version for two is possible. After passing out the envelopes, the performer introduces a medium, blindfolds her and leaves for a position behind the curtain where he can see the audience and whisper to the medium.

She directs the sealing and collecting of the envelopes. She sees the key number each time by looking down the blindfold, cues the performer with a simple finger code and he gives her a description of the owner with details of clothes and appearance.

66. GRAPHOLOGY

Handwriting is something which may or may not identify one person from another. It has been claimed that a good handwriting analyst or graphologist can collect handwritten notes from 15 different people, examine the writing on any random note and hand the note back to its owner. This works, so the claim goes, even if the person disguises his handwriting.

L. Vosburgh Lyons used this premise for a test in handwriting analysis. The following is a modified version of his routine. It is excellent for any group, from a small party of 5 to an auditorium of hundreds.

Each of 10 to 20 persons is handed a slip of paper and a pencil or pen. On getting a piece of paper, each person writes a sentence. It can be a quote from some famous work or a more mundane entry such as directions for baking a cake. The performer turns his back or leaves the room during the interval when the papers are collected and mixed an any acceptable container.

Then the performer returns to the scene. Reaching into the papers, he looks at each and proceeds to gaze over those watching him. Then he deliberately approaches one person and gives him the writing. He is always correct. This action is continued until all present are handed back their slip of paper.

METHOD: After the Annemann trick was published, many

magicians devised variations. The Lyons routine is one of the best. It used a system where blank business cards were handed to each of 20 people. Each card was edge marked with a pencil to distinguish it from the other cards.

The easiest system is the Annemann method described in the previous trick. Here you have each person write something on a slip of paper, fold the paper and seal it in an envelope. The inside of each envelope is of course marked with a lightly written number and the numbers run consecutively from 1 to 20.

Distribute the envelopes in numerical order, along with slips of paper and pencils. Once the spectators have written something on their slips, folded the slips and sealed them in the envelopes, it remains only to have the envelopes collected and mixed. You then pick up a random envelope, open it, pretend to analyze the handwriting on the slip and identify the person who did the writing.

67. SUPER PSYCHOMETRY

This routine is the last in the book. It is also the longest and the most carefully detailed. In it you will find elements of psychometry, cold reading and telepathy. To the average audience it is a staggering demonstration of paranormal ability, an overwhelmingly positive test that ESP exists.

The secret of the routine is basically simple. You can absorb the material in one reading. But the routine is open-ended as well. This means that there is no single procedure to follow each time the trick is performed. As you become more experienced with this routine, you will pick up many ideas that will add to the authenticity of the demonstration. Some of this inside information will be discussed here so you will know what to look for in future performances.

Envelopes and pencils are handed out to about 10 people in the audience. On the outside of each envelope the performer has written three questions. The first is "What's your favorite TV show?" The second is "Who would you like to be?" The third question varies. On one envelope it may be "What's your lucky number?" On another "How much change do you have?" On another "What is the month and day of your birthday?" On another "What kind of car do you drive?"

Each person is told to jot down an answer to each question on the outside of his envelope. Then each person drops some small possession into his or her envelope. The envelopes are sealed, gathered in a hat, mixed and tossed out onto the table.

The mentalist places one sealed envelope aside under the hat. No one, including the mentalist, knows what is written on the envelope or what is inside it.

From here the mentalist proceeds to pick a random envelope, study the questions and answers on the outside and then verbally describe the type of person who would give these answers. He opens the envelope, removes the object, offers a more detailed description of the owner and then returns the object to its rightful owner.

This may seem to be little more than the psychometry test described at the beginning of this chapter, but it is far more elaborate. The mentalist not only describes the owner's appearance and attire, he describes the person's character. He can even tell, on occasion, if the person is left-handed or right-handed, if the person smokes cigarettes, cigars or a pipe, give horoscope readings and so on, without knowing who the person is. All information is pertinent and completely accurate even though the mentalist has never seen the spectators before.

To complete the test, after the mentalist has returned all borrowed articles to their owners, he reminds the audience that there is still one more sealed envelope and that it is hidden under the hat. No one, except the owner of the envelope, knows what was written on the outside of the envelope.

"Obviously I know the identity of the gentleman who filled out the information on this last envelope because he is the only spectator remaining. So I will not tell him who he is. Rather, I'll try to describe things about him that I would not be likely to know."

Here the mentalist gives a cold reading—that is, he tells the person about his character, his likes and dislikes, and even the data of his birth. Then he astounds the audience by telling the spectator exactly how much change he has in his pocket!

METHOD: The basic approach is the Annemann idea described at the beginning of this chapter. Each envelope is secretly marked on the inside with a number. Since the envelopes are handed out in numerical order, once you know that an envelope is, say, the fifth envelope, then you know that the content of the envelope (and the information written on the outside of the envelope) belongs to the fifth spectator.

This tells you the identity of the correct person but it tells you nothing *about* that person. It is the information on the outside of the envelope that gives you apparent clues about the spectator's character.

Each person thinks that he is unique. If he tells you his favorite TV show, he thinks he is telling you about himself. When you read his answer to the question, "What is your favorite TV show?" act as if the answer is important. If it is a comedy show, say, "This is a person who has a keen sense of humor, who enjoys a good joke and appreciates the humor in a situation." This may seem quite specific, but it is the sort of statement that fits almost anyone.

What is at work here is a technique known as cold reading, that is, the ability to tell someone about himself the instant you meet him. It is a technique that comes with experience. You have considerable help with this routine because there are questions and answers on the envelope. Just be sure to keep your comments vague and positive. If your flatter someone, he can hardly disagree with your evaluation of him. In a nutshell, tell people what they want to hear.

The second question on the outside of each envelope is, "Who would you like to be?" The answer can be a celebrity, a politician, a historical figure, even an athelete, a general or a character from fiction.

The answers you get generally allow for comedy interludes. Thus, a small meek individual may admit that he'd like to be Napoleon. Do not make fun of the person. Instead, say, "This is an individual who would like to be a world leader, who keeps up on current events, who is a student of history and has an insight into the structure of power." Again this seems specific, but it is really a general comment that fits almost anyone.

The third question can be anything. You can use favorite color on one envelope, lucky number on another, and so on. These add variety, but they serve a more important function. After the show, people will leave with the impression that you told *every* participant his date of birth, his lucky number, etc.

The last item we need to consider is the content of individual envelopes. In time, as you gain experience with this type of routine, you will add to your storehouse of knowledge about human behavior and personality. For the purpose of this book, we will suggest a few things that will indicate how much information you can gain from ordinary and quite mundane objects. For our example we will use a packet of matches.

When you tear open an envelope and find a packet of matches inside, you simultaneously glimpse the secret number written inside the envelope. This tells you exactly who in the audience was given this envelope. Whereas you had to be somewhat general about the person's identity when studying the answers to the questions on the outside of the envelope, now you can be completely accurate.

In our example, the object is a book of matches. Hold the matches to your forehead as if trying to receive a mental impression. In fact what you do is determine if the matchbook has a slight odor of perfume or tobacco. If the packet smells of perfume, you know the matches belong to a woman. You have not yet glanced at the audience, but you know the book belongs to a woman. If there is a slight tobacco odor, the person smokes.

If the matchbook smells of cigar or pipe tobacco, you know that the spectator is an adult male. Pipe tobaccos have distinctive odors. You can, with a modicum of practice, identify major brand-name tobaccos by the slight odor.

By the same reasoning, and this too comes with experience, you can tell if the odor is from perfume, cologne, or cosmetics. If you know a bit about perfume you can, at times, tell the brand name.

If someone gives you a book of matches, you know that person is *not* a compulsive smoker. If they were, they would not relinquish their matches to anyone. So you also know that if the person smokes, he smokes in moderation.

Open the matchbook. If matches have been removed from the right side, as is usually the case, you know the person is right-handed. But if matches have been removed from the left side, you know the person is left-handed.

Note also if there is advertising matter on the matchbook. If the ad is not a general one from a national advertiser, if it is local and refers to a local nightclub or restaurant, you know the spectator probably got the matches from that restaurant.

Now step back and take a look at all the information you could have gotten from a book of matches. At a glance you know that it came from a left-handed cigarette-smoking woman who uses French perfume and likes Chinese food. You can see that this information can be made the starting point for an astounding reading about a person you've never seen before.

On several envelopes arrange to have a question asking for the month and day of a person's birthday. To prepare for the answer to this question, get any popular book on astrology and learn the pitch for the twelve signs of the zodiac. Most people know a little about the sign they were born under. Your small investment in time spent learning the signs of the zodiac will repay you many times over in the reputation you will gain as an astrologer.

An important tip. Do not reveal astrological information when you read the answers on the outside of the envelope. Wait until you have removed the object from the envelope. You thus pretend to get the information *from the object* and not from the envelope.

There is one final note. This type of test is very impressive to the audience because when you hand out envelopes and pencils, the *only* people who know what you've written on the envelopes are the people who get envelopes. The *only* people who know that they have given you information about themselves are the people who answer the questions on the envelopes. The rest of the audience is vaguely aware that envelopes are being passed out and collected, but they have no clear idea of exactly what is going on.

This means that if you reveal someone's astrological sign, *most* of the people in the audience do not know you got this information from an envelope. They think you read the volunteer's mind and they will be amazed that you can read the minds of many volunteers with complete accuracy. In other words, the majority of the audience will give your credit for tremendous mental powers because all they see is a mentalist onstage giving an enormous amount of accurate information about people he has never met before.

The most impressive part of "Super Psychometry" is the one

you use to finish the routine. This is the test where you have one person left and you tell him the amount of change in his pocket. His sealed envelope is hidden under the hat. You do not touch the envelope. Facing the spectator, you tell him about himself, then you go on to tell him how much change he has in his pocket. In any psychic setting the most memorable tests are those with a strong finish. The finish to "Super Psychometry" is a knockout because it cannot be explained by any rational means.

This final test is set up as follows. One envelope is reserved for the test. On the outside you write three questions. The first two questions are about the spectator's favorite TV show and the month and day of his birth. The third question is, "How much change do you have in your pocket?"

Give this envelope to a man rather than a woman. It is easier for a man to remove the change from his trouser pocket than it is for a woman to get the change out of a small purse in her pocketbook. Don't pick a wealthy-looking individual because he probably carries credit cards and no change. Even then, if the person you pick says he has no change, ask him to jot down how much he has in paper money.

After all the participants have answered the questions on the outside of their envelopes and sealed an object in the envelopes, pick up an ordinary hat and use it to collect the sealed envelopes.

Take each envelope from each person and drop it into the hat. Hold the hat up high so it is above the eye level of the spectators. When you take the envelope from the gentleman who wrote the amount of change in his pocket, grasp it with the right hand and place it into the hat where it is held in place by the left hand, Figure 71. Look away as you take each envelope, so it is clear to the audience that you don't see the writing on the outside of the envelope.

Collect the remaining envelopes. Then go back to the stage. Mix the envelopes around in the hat without letting go of the envelope which your left hand grasps. Turn the left hand (and the hat) around to the position shown in Figure 72 as you begin to dump the envelopes out onto the table. The writing on the key envelope is facing you and you can see it at a glance. Memorize each of the three answers on the envelope.

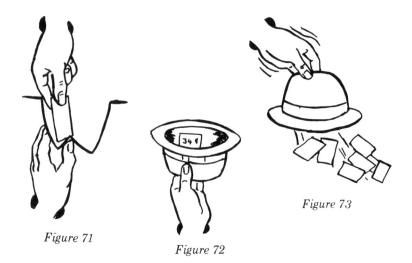

Figure 71

Figure 72

Figure 73

Immediately dump the contents of the hat out on the table, Figure 73. Look away as you do this, making it clear that you don't see the writing on any envelope yet. Don't release the left-hand grip on the envelope still inside the hat.

Place the hat brim-down over the envelopes. Pretend to slide the envelopes around with your right hand, mixing them sight unseen. Explain to the audience that you want to select one envelope at random and hide it under the hat until the end of the experiment.

Release your left hand's grasp on the envelope inside the hat and take it with the right hand. The hands slide to the side with the hat so that the hat is now some distance away from the pile of envelopes. As seen by the audience, you have gathered a hat-ful of sealed envelopes from the audience, dumped the hat brim down on the table, taken an envelope at random and placed it under the hat. The hat, with the envelope underneath, is now on the table, brim-down, some distance away from the pile of envelopes.

Now proceed with the routine as described above. Pick up a random envelope, read the answers aloud and pretend they have significance. Open the envelope, study the object, tell the person something about himself or herself, then hand the object back to its owner. Do this with all of the visible envelopes in the heap on the table. It is easier to have all the participants stand.

As you return each article, the participant sits down. Continue with all of the volunteers until just one is left standing.

This spectator is the one whose envelope is under the hat. Explain that you have neither seen nor touched the envelope. You don't know what's written on it. You then proceed to read his mind, give him a character reading and reveal his zodiac sign. Finish by telling him how much change he has in his pocket.

A CATALOG OF SELECTED
DOVER BOOKS
IN ALL FIELDS OF INTEREST

A CATALOG OF SELECTED DOVER
BOOKS IN ALL FIELDS OF INTEREST

CONCERNING THE SPIRITUAL IN ART, Wassily Kandinsky. Pioneering work by father of abstract art. Thoughts on color theory, nature of art. Analysis of earlier masters. 12 illustrations. 80pp. of text. 5⅜ x 8½. 0-486-23411-8

CELTIC ART: The Methods of Construction, George Bain. Simple geometric techniques for making Celtic interlacements, spirals, Kells-type initials, animals, humans, etc. Over 500 illustrations. 160pp. 9 x 12. (Available in U.S. only.) 0-486-22923-8

AN ATLAS OF ANATOMY FOR ARTISTS, Fritz Schider. Most thorough reference work on art anatomy in the world. Hundreds of illustrations, including selections from works by Vesalius, Leonardo, Goya, Ingres, Michelangelo, others. 593 illustrations. 192pp. 7⅛ x 10¼. 0-486-20241-0

CELTIC HAND STROKE-BY-STROKE (Irish Half-Uncial from "The Book of Kells"): An Arthur Baker Calligraphy Manual, Arthur Baker. Complete guide to creating each letter of the alphabet in distinctive Celtic manner. Covers hand position, strokes, pens, inks, paper, more. Illustrated. 48pp. 8¼ x 11. 0-486-24336-2

EASY ORIGAMI, John Montroll. Charming collection of 32 projects (hat, cup, pelican, piano, swan, many more) specially designed for the novice origami hobbyist. Clearly illustrated easy-to-follow instructions insure that even beginning papercrafters will achieve successful results. 48pp. 8¼ x 11. 0-486-27298-2

BLOOMINGDALE'S ILLUSTRATED 1886 CATALOG: Fashions, Dry Goods and Housewares, Bloomingdale Brothers. Famed merchants' extremely rare catalog depicting about 1,700 products: clothing, housewares, firearms, dry goods, jewelry, more. Invaluable for dating, identifying vintage items. Also, copyright-free graphics for artists, designers. Co-published with Henry Ford Museum & Greenfield Village. 160pp. 8¼ x 11. 0-486-25780-0

THE ART OF WORLDLY WISDOM, Baltasar Gracian. "Think with the few and speak with the many," "Friends are a second existence," and "Be able to forget" are among this 1637 volume's 300 pithy maxims. A perfect source of mental and spiritual refreshment, it can be opened at random and appreciated either in brief or at length. 128pp. 5⅜ x 8½. 0-486-44034-6

JOHNSON'S DICTIONARY: A Modern Selection, Samuel Johnson (E. L. McAdam and George Milne, eds.). This modern version reduces the original 1755 edition's 2,300 pages of definitions and literary examples to a more manageable length, retaining the verbal pleasure and historical curiosity of the original. 480pp. 5⁹⁄₁₆ x 8¼. 0-486-44089-3

ADVENTURES OF HUCKLEBERRY FINN, Mark Twain, Illustrated by E. W. Kemble. A work of eternal richness and complexity, a source of ongoing critical debate, and a literary landmark, Twain's 1885 masterpiece about a barefoot boy's journey of self-discovery has enthralled readers around the world. This handsome clothbound reproduction of the first edition features all 174 of the original black-and-white illustrations. 368pp. 5⅜ x 8½. 0-486-44322-1

CATALOG OF DOVER BOOKS

STICKLEY CRAFTSMAN FURNITURE CATALOGS, Gustav Stickley and L. & J. G. Stickley. Beautiful, functional furniture in two authentic catalogs from 1910. 594 illustrations, including 277 photos, show settles, rockers, armchairs, reclining chairs, bookcases, desks, tables. 183pp. 6½ x 9¼.   0-486-23838-5

AMERICAN LOCOMOTIVES IN HISTORIC PHOTOGRAPHS: 1858 to 1949, Ron Ziel (ed.). A rare collection of 126 meticulously detailed official photographs, called "builder portraits," of American locomotives that majestically chronicle the rise of steam locomotive power in America. Introduction. Detailed captions. xi+ 129pp. 9 x 12.   0-486-27393-8

AMERICA'S LIGHTHOUSES: An Illustrated History, Francis Ross Holland, Jr. Delightfully written, profusely illustrated fact-filled survey of over 200 American light-houses since 1716. History, anecdotes, technological advances, more. 240pp. 8 x 10¾.
0-486-25576-X

TOWARDS A NEW ARCHITECTURE, Le Corbusier. Pioneering manifesto by founder of "International School." Technical and aesthetic theories, views of industry, eco-nomics, relation of form to function, "mass-production split" and much more. Profusely illustrated. 320pp. 6⅛ x 9¼. (Available in U.S. only.)   0-486-25023-7

HOW THE OTHER HALF LIVES, Jacob Riis. Famous journalistic record, expos-ing poverty and degradation of New York slums around 1900, by major social reformer. 100 striking and influential photographs. 233pp. 10 x 7⅞.   0-486-22012-5

FRUIT KEY AND TWIG KEY TO TREES AND SHRUBS, William M. Harlow. One of the handiest and most widely used identification aids. Fruit key covers 120 deciduous and evergreen species; twig key 160 deciduous species. Easily used. Over 300 photographs. 126pp. 5⅜ x 8½.   0-486-20511-8

COMMON BIRD SONGS, Dr. Donald J. Borror. Songs of 60 most common U.S. birds: robins, sparrows, cardinals, bluejays, finches, more–arranged in order of increasing complexity. Up to 9 variations of songs of each species.
Cassette and manual 0-486-99911-4

ORCHIDS AS HOUSE PLANTS, Rebecca Tyson Northen. Grow cattleyas and many other kinds of orchids–in a window, in a case, or under artificial light. 63 illus-trations. 148pp. 5⅜ x 8½.   0-486-23261-1

MONSTER MAZES, Dave Phillips. Masterful mazes at four levels of difficulty. Avoid deadly perils and evil creatures to find magical treasures. Solutions for all 32 exciting illustrated puzzles. 48pp. 8¼ x 11.   0-486-26005-4

MOZART'S DON GIOVANNI (DOVER OPERA LIBRETTO SERIES), Wolfgang Amadeus Mozart. Introduced and translated by Ellen H. Bleiler. Standard Italian libretto, with complete English translation. Convenient and thoroughly portable–an ideal companion for reading along with a recording or the performance itself. Introduction. List of characters. Plot summary. 121pp. 5¼ x 8½. 0-486-24944-1

FRANK LLOYD WRIGHT'S DANA HOUSE, Donald Hoffmann. Pictorial essay of residential masterpiece with over 160 interior and exterior photos, plans, eleva-tions, sketches and studies. 128pp. 9¹/₄ x 10¾.   0-486-29120-0

THE CLARINET AND CLARINET PLAYING, David Pino. Lively, comprehensive work features suggestions about technique, musicianship, and musical interpretation, as well as guidelines for teaching, making your own reeds, and preparing for public performance. Includes an intriguing look at clarinet history. "A godsend," *The Clarinet,* Journal of the International Clarinet Society. Appendixes. 7 illus. 320pp. 5⅜ x 8½. 0-486-40270-3

HOLLYWOOD GLAMOR PORTRAITS, John Kobal (ed.). 145 photos from 1926-49. Harlow, Gable, Bogart, Bacall; 94 stars in all. Full background on photographers, technical aspects. 160pp. 8⅜ x 11¼. 0-486-23352-9

THE RAVEN AND OTHER FAVORITE POEMS, Edgar Allan Poe. Over 40 of the author's most memorable poems: "The Bells," "Ulalume," "Israfel," "To Helen," "The Conqueror Worm," "Eldorado," "Annabel Lee," many more. Alphabetic lists of titles and first lines. 64pp. 5³⁄₁₆ x 8¼. 0-486-26685-0

PERSONAL MEMOIRS OF U. S. GRANT, Ulysses Simpson Grant. Intelligent, deeply moving firsthand account of Civil War campaigns, considered by many the finest military memoirs ever written. Includes letters, historic photographs, maps and more. 528pp. 6⅛ x 9¼. 0-486-28587-1

ANCIENT EGYPTIAN MATERIALS AND INDUSTRIES, A. Lucas and J. Harris. Fascinating, comprehensive, thoroughly documented text describes this ancient civilization's vast resources and the processes that incorporated them in daily life, including the use of animal products, building materials, cosmetics, perfumes and incense, fibers, glazed ware, glass and its manufacture, materials used in the mummification process, and much more. 544pp. 6⅛ x 9¼. (Available in U.S. only.) 0-486-40446-3

RUSSIAN STORIES/RUSSKIE RASSKAZY: A Dual-Language Book, edited by Gleb Struve. Twelve tales by such masters as Chekhov, Tolstoy, Dostoevsky, Pushkin, others. Excellent word-for-word English translations on facing pages, plus teaching and study aids, Russian/English vocabulary, biographical/critical introductions, more. 416pp. 5⅜ x 8½. 0-486-26244-8

PHILADELPHIA THEN AND NOW: 60 Sites Photographed in the Past and Present, Kenneth Finkel and Susan Oyama. Rare photographs of City Hall, Logan Square, Independence Hall, Betsy Ross House, other landmarks juxtaposed with contemporary views. Captures changing face of historic city. Introduction. Captions. 128pp. 8¼ x 11. 0-486-25790-8

NORTH AMERICAN INDIAN LIFE: Customs and Traditions of 23 Tribes, Elsie Clews Parsons (ed.). 27 fictionalized essays by noted anthropologists examine religion, customs, government, additional facets of life among the Winnebago, Crow, Zuni, Eskimo, other tribes. 480pp. 6⅛ x 9¼. 0-486-27377-6

TECHNICAL MANUAL AND DICTIONARY OF CLASSICAL BALLET, Gail Grant. Defines, explains, comments on steps, movements, poses and concepts. 15-page pictorial section. Basic book for student, viewer. 127pp. 5⅜ x 8½. 0-486-21843-0

THE MALE AND FEMALE FIGURE IN MOTION: 60 Classic Photographic Sequences, Eadweard Muybridge. 60 true-action photographs of men and women walking, running, climbing, bending, turning, etc., reproduced from rare 19th-century masterpiece. vi + 121pp. 9 x 12. 0-486-24745-7

ANIMALS: 1,419 Copyright-Free Illustrations of Mammals, Birds, Fish, Insects, etc., Jim Harter (ed.). Clear wood engravings present, in extremely lifelike poses, over 1,000 species of animals. One of the most extensive pictorial sourcebooks of its kind. Captions. Index. 284pp. 9 x 12.　　　　　　　　　　　　　　0-486-23766-4

1001 QUESTIONS ANSWERED ABOUT THE SEASHORE, N. J. Berrill and Jacquelyn Berrill. Queries answered about dolphins, sea snails, sponges, starfish, fishes, shore birds, many others. Covers appearance, breeding, growth, feeding, much more. 305pp. 5¼ x 8¼.　　　　　　　　　　　　　　　0-486-23366-9

ATTRACTING BIRDS TO YOUR YARD, William J. Weber. Easy-to-follow guide offers advice on how to attract the greatest diversity of birds: birdhouses, feeders, water and waterers, much more. 96pp. 5³/₁₆ x 8¼.　　　　　　　　0-486-28927-3

MEDICINAL AND OTHER USES OF NORTH AMERICAN PLANTS: A Historical Survey with Special Reference to the Eastern Indian Tribes, Charlotte Erichsen-Brown. Chronological historical citations document 500 years of usage of plants, trees, shrubs native to eastern Canada, northeastern U.S. Also complete identifying information. 343 illustrations. 544pp. 6½ x 9¼.　　　　0-486-25951-X

STORYBOOK MAZES, Dave Phillips. 23 stories and mazes on two-page spreads: Wizard of Oz, Treasure Island, Robin Hood, etc. Solutions. 64pp. 8¼ x 11.
　　　　　　　　　　　　　　　　　　　　　　　　　0-486-23628-5

AMERICAN NEGRO SONGS: 230 Folk Songs and Spirituals, Religious and Secular, John W. Work. This authoritative study traces the African influences of songs sung and played by black Americans at work, in church, and as entertainment. The author discusses the lyric significance of such songs as "Swing Low, Sweet Chariot," "John Henry," and others and offers the words and music for 230 songs. Bibliography. Index of Song Titles. 272pp. 6½ x 9¼.　　　　　0-486-40271-1

MOVIE-STAR PORTRAITS OF THE FORTIES, John Kobal (ed.). 163 glamor, studio photos of 106 stars of the 1940s: Rita Hayworth, Ava Gardner, Marlon Brando, Clark Gable, many more. 176pp. 8⅜ x 11¼.　　　　　　0-486-23546-7

YEKL and THE IMPORTED BRIDEGROOM AND OTHER STORIES OF YIDDISH NEW YORK, Abraham Cahan. Film Hester Street based on *Yekl* (1896). Novel, other stories among first about Jewish immigrants on N.Y.'s East Side. 240pp. 5⅜ x 8½.　　　　　　　　　　　　　　　　　　0-486-22427-9

SELECTED POEMS, Walt Whitman. Generous sampling from *Leaves of Grass*. Twenty-four poems include "I Hear America Singing," "Song of the Open Road," "I Sing the Body Electric," "When Lilacs Last in the Dooryard Bloom'd," "O Captain! My Captain!"–all reprinted from an authoritative edition. Lists of titles and first lines. 128pp. 5³/₁₆ x 8¼.　　　　　　　　　　　　　　0-486-26878-0

SONGS OF EXPERIENCE: Facsimile Reproduction with 26 Plates in Full Color, William Blake. 26 full-color plates from a rare 1826 edition. Includes "The Tyger," "London," "Holy Thursday," and other poems. Printed text of poems. 48pp. 5¼ x 7.
　　　　　　　　　　　　　　　　　　　　　　　　　0-486-24636-1

THE BEST TALES OF HOFFMANN, E. T. A. Hoffmann. 10 of Hoffmann's most important stories: "Nutcracker and the King of Mice," "The Golden Flowerpot," etc. 458pp. 5⅜ x 8½.　　　　　　　　　　　　　　　　　0-486-21793-0

THE BOOK OF TEA, Kakuzo Okakura. Minor classic of the Orient: entertaining, charming explanation, interpretation of traditional Japanese culture in terms of tea ceremony. 94pp. 5⅜ x 8½.　　　　　　　　　　　　　　0-486-20070-1

FRENCH STORIES/CONTES FRANÇAIS: A Dual-Language Book, Wallace Fowlie. Ten stories by French masters, Voltaire to Camus: "Micromegas" by Voltaire; "The Atheist's Mass" by Balzac; "Minuet" by de Maupassant; "The Guest" by Camus, six more. Excellent English translations on facing pages. Also French-English vocabulary list, exercises, more. 352pp. 5⅜ x 8½. 0-486-26443-2

CHICAGO AT THE TURN OF THE CENTURY IN PHOTOGRAPHS: 122 Historic Views from the Collections of the Chicago Historical Society, Larry A. Viskochil. Rare large-format prints offer detailed views of City Hall, State Street, the Loop, Hull House, Union Station, many other landmarks, circa 1904-1913. Introduction. Captions. Maps. 144pp. 9⅜ x 12¼. 0-486-24656-6

OLD BROOKLYN IN EARLY PHOTOGRAPHS, 1865-1929, William Lee Younger. Luna Park, Gravesend race track, construction of Grand Army Plaza, moving of Hotel Brighton, etc. 157 previously unpublished photographs. 165pp. 8⅞ x 11¾. 0-486-23587-4

THE MYTHS OF THE NORTH AMERICAN INDIANS, Lewis Spence. Rich anthology of the myths and legends of the Algonquins, Iroquois, Pawnees and Sioux, prefaced by an extensive historical and ethnological commentary. 36 illustrations. 480pp. 5⅜ x 8½. 0-486-25967-6

AN ENCYCLOPEDIA OF BATTLES: Accounts of Over 1,560 Battles from 1479 B.C. to the Present, David Eggenberger. Essential details of every major battle in recorded history from the first battle of Megiddo in 1479 B.C. to Grenada in 1984. List of Battle Maps. New Appendix covering the years 1967-1984. Index. 99 illustrations. 544pp. 6½ x 9¼. 0-486-24913-1

SAILING ALONE AROUND THE WORLD, Captain Joshua Slocum. First man to sail around the world, alone, in small boat. One of great feats of seamanship told in delightful manner. 67 illustrations. 294pp. 5⅜ x 8½. 0-486-20326-3

ANARCHISM AND OTHER ESSAYS, Emma Goldman. Powerful, penetrating, prophetic essays on direct action, role of minorities, prison reform, puritan hypocrisy, violence, etc. 271pp. 5⅜ x 8½. 0-486-22484-8

MYTHS OF THE HINDUS AND BUDDHISTS, Ananda K. Coomaraswamy and Sister Nivedita. Great stories of the epics; deeds of Krishna, Shiva, taken from puranas, Vedas, folk tales; etc. 32 illustrations. 400pp. 5⅜ x 8½. 0-486-21759-0

MY BONDAGE AND MY FREEDOM, Frederick Douglass. Born a slave, Douglass became outspoken force in antislavery movement. The best of Douglass' autobiographies. Graphic description of slave life. 464pp. 5⅜ x 8½. 0-486-22457-0

FOLLOWING THE EQUATOR: A Journey Around the World, Mark Twain. Fascinating humorous account of 1897 voyage to Hawaii, Australia, India, New Zealand, etc. Ironic, bemused reports on peoples, customs, climate, flora and fauna, politics, much more. 197 illustrations. 720pp. 5⅜ x 8½. 0-486-26113-1

THE PEOPLE CALLED SHAKERS, Edward D. Andrews. Definitive study of Shakers: origins, beliefs, practices, dances, social organization, furniture and crafts, etc. 33 illustrations. 351pp. 5⅜ x 8½. 0-486-21081-2

THE MYTHS OF GREECE AND ROME, H. A. Guerber. A classic of mythology, generously illustrated, long prized for its simple, graphic, accurate retelling of the principal myths of Greece and Rome, and for its commentary on their origins and significance. With 64 illustrations by Michelangelo, Raphael, Titian, Rubens, Canova, Bernini and others. 480pp. 5⅜ x 8½. 0-486-27584-1

PSYCHOLOGY OF MUSIC, Carl E. Seashore. Classic work discusses music as a medium from psychological viewpoint. Clear treatment of physical acoustics, auditory apparatus, sound perception, development of musical skills, nature of musical feeling, host of other topics. 88 figures. 408pp. 5⅜ x 8½. 0-486-21851-1

LIFE IN ANCIENT EGYPT, Adolf Erman. Fullest, most thorough, detailed older account with much not in more recent books, domestic life, religion, magic, medicine, commerce, much more. Many illustrations reproduce tomb paintings, carvings, hieroglyphs, etc. 597pp. 5⅜ x 8½. 0-486-22632-8

SUNDIALS, Their Theory and Construction, Albert Waugh. Far and away the best, most thorough coverage of ideas, mathematics concerned, types, construction, adjusting anywhere. Simple, nontechnical treatment allows even children to build several of these dials. Over 100 illustrations. 230pp. 5⅜ x 8½. 0-486-22947-5

THEORETICAL HYDRODYNAMICS, L. M. Milne-Thomson. Classic exposition of the mathematical theory of fluid motion, applicable to both hydrodynamics and aerodynamics. Over 600 exercises. 768pp. 6⅛ x 9¼. 0-486-68970-0

OLD-TIME VIGNETTES IN FULL COLOR, Carol Belanger Grafton (ed.). Over 390 charming, often sentimental illustrations, selected from archives of Victorian graphics–pretty women posing, children playing, food, flowers, kittens and puppies, smiling cherubs, birds and butterflies, much more. All copyright-free. 48pp. 9¼ x 12¼. 0-486-27269-9

PERSPECTIVE FOR ARTISTS, Rex Vicat Cole. Depth, perspective of sky and sea, shadows, much more, not usually covered. 391 diagrams, 81 reproductions of drawings and paintings. 279pp. 5⅜ x 8½. 0-486-22487-2

DRAWING THE LIVING FIGURE, Joseph Sheppard. Innovative approach to artistic anatomy focuses on specifics of surface anatomy, rather than muscles and bones. Over 170 drawings of live models in front, back and side views, and in widely varying poses. Accompanying diagrams. 177 illustrations. Introduction. Index. 144pp. 8⅜ x11¼. 0-486-26723-7

GOTHIC AND OLD ENGLISH ALPHABETS: 100 Complete Fonts, Dan X. Solo. Add power, elegance to posters, signs, other graphics with 100 stunning copyright-free alphabets: Blackstone, Dolbey, Germania, 97 more–including many lower-case, numerals, punctuation marks. 104pp. 8⅛ x 11. 0-486-24695-7

THE BOOK OF WOOD CARVING, Charles Marshall Sayers. Finest book for beginners discusses fundamentals and offers 34 designs. "Absolutely first rate . . . well thought out and well executed."–E. J. Tangerman. 118pp. 7¾ x 10⅝. 0-486-23654-4

ILLUSTRATED CATALOG OF CIVIL WAR MILITARY GOODS: Union Army Weapons, Insignia, Uniform Accessories, and Other Equipment, Schuyler, Hartley, and Graham. Rare, profusely illustrated 1846 catalog includes Union Army uniform and dress regulations, arms and ammunition, coats, insignia, flags, swords, rifles, etc. 226 illustrations. 160pp. 9 x 12. 0-486-24939-5

WOMEN'S FASHIONS OF THE EARLY 1900s: An Unabridged Republication of "New York Fashions, 1909," National Cloak & Suit Co. Rare catalog of mail-order fashions documents women's and children's clothing styles shortly after the turn of the century. Captions offer full descriptions, prices. Invaluable resource for fashion, costume historians. Approximately 725 illustrations. 128pp. 8⅜ x 11¼. 0-486-27276-1

HOW TO DO BEADWORK, Mary White. Fundamental book on craft from simple projects to five-bead chains and woven works. 106 illustrations. 142pp. 5⅜ x 8. 0-486-20697-1

THE 1912 AND 1915 GUSTAV STICKLEY FURNITURE CATALOGS, Gustav Stickley. With over 200 detailed illustrations and descriptions, these two catalogs are essential reading and reference materials and identification guides for Stickley furniture. Captions cite materials, dimensions and prices. 112pp. 6½ x 9¼. 0-486-26676-1

EARLY AMERICAN LOCOMOTIVES, John H. White, Jr. Finest locomotive engravings from early 19th century: historical (1804–74), main-line (after 1870), special, foreign, etc. 147 plates. 142pp. 11⅜ x 8¼. 0-486-22772-3

LITTLE BOOK OF EARLY AMERICAN CRAFTS AND TRADES, Peter Stockham (ed.). 1807 children's book explains crafts and trades: baker, hatter, cooper, potter, and many others. 23 copperplate illustrations. 140pp. 4⅝ x 6. 0-486-23336-7

VICTORIAN FASHIONS AND COSTUMES FROM HARPER'S BAZAR, 1867–1898, Stella Blum (ed.). Day costumes, evening wear, sports clothes, shoes, hats, other accessories in over 1,000 detailed engravings. 320pp. 9⅜ x 12¼. 0-486-22990-4

THE LONG ISLAND RAIL ROAD IN EARLY PHOTOGRAPHS, Ron Ziel. Over 220 rare photos, informative text document origin (1844) and development of rail service on Long Island. Vintage views of early trains, locomotives, stations, passengers, crews, much more. Captions. 8⅞ x 11¾. 0-486-26301-0

VOYAGE OF THE LIBERDADE, Joshua Slocum. Great 19th-century mariner's thrilling, first-hand account of the wreck of his ship off South America, the 35-foot boat he built from the wreckage, and its remarkable voyage home. 128pp. 5⅜ x 8½. 0-486-40022-0

TEN BOOKS ON ARCHITECTURE, Vitruvius. The most important book ever written on architecture. Early Roman aesthetics, technology, classical orders, site selection, all other aspects. Morgan translation. 331pp. 5⅜ x 8½. 0-486-20645-9

THE HUMAN FIGURE IN MOTION, Eadweard Muybridge. More than 4,500 stopped-action photos, in action series, showing undraped men, women, children jumping, lying down, throwing, sitting, wrestling, carrying, etc. 390pp. 7⅞ x 10⅝. 0-486-20204-6 Clothbd.

TREES OF THE EASTERN AND CENTRAL UNITED STATES AND CANADA, William M. Harlow. Best one-volume guide to 140 trees. Full descriptions, woodlore, range, etc. Over 600 illustrations. Handy size. 288pp. 4½ x 6⅜. 0-486-20395-6

GROWING AND USING HERBS AND SPICES, Milo Miloradovich. Versatile handbook provides all the information needed for cultivation and use of all the herbs and spices available in North America. 4 illustrations. Index. Glossary. 236pp. 5⅜ x 8½. 0-486-25058-X

BIG BOOK OF MAZES AND LABYRINTHS, Walter Shepherd. 50 mazes and labyrinths in all–classical, solid, ripple, and more–in one great volume. Perfect inexpensive puzzler for clever youngsters. Full solutions. 112pp. 8⅛ x 11. 0-486-22951-3

PIANO TUNING, J. Cree Fischer. Clearest, best book for beginner, amateur. Simple repairs, raising dropped notes, tuning by easy method of flattened fifths. No previous skills needed. 4 illustrations. 201pp. 5⅜ x 8½. 0-486-23267-0

HINTS TO SINGERS, Lillian Nordica. Selecting the right teacher, developing confidence, overcoming stage fright, and many other important skills receive thoughtful discussion in this indispensible guide, written by a world-famous diva of four decades' experience. 96pp. 5⅜ x 8½. 0-486-40094-8

THE COMPLETE NONSENSE OF EDWARD LEAR, Edward Lear. All nonsense limericks, zany alphabets, Owl and Pussycat, songs, nonsense botany, etc., illustrated by Lear. Total of 320pp. 5⅜ x 8½. (Available in U.S. only.) 0-486-20167-8

VICTORIAN PARLOUR POETRY: An Annotated Anthology, Michael R. Turner. 117 gems by Longfellow, Tennyson, Browning, many lesser-known poets. "The Village Blacksmith," "Curfew Must Not Ring Tonight," "Only a Baby Small," dozens more, often difficult to find elsewhere. Index of poets, titles, first lines. xxiii + 325pp. 5⅝ x 8¼. 0-486-27044-0

DUBLINERS, James Joyce. Fifteen stories offer vivid, tightly focused observations of the lives of Dublin's poorer classes. At least one, "The Dead," is considered a masterpiece. Reprinted complete and unabridged from standard edition. 160pp. $5\frac{3}{16}$ x 8¼. 0-486-26870-5

GREAT WEIRD TALES: 14 Stories by Lovecraft, Blackwood, Machen and Others, S. T. Joshi (ed.). 14 spellbinding tales, including "The Sin Eater," by Fiona McLeod, "The Eye Above the Mantel," by Frank Belknap Long, as well as renowned works by R. H. Barlow, Lord Dunsany, Arthur Machen, W. C. Morrow and eight other masters of the genre. 256pp. 5⅜ x 8½. (Available in U.S. only.) 0-486-40436-6

THE BOOK OF THE SACRED MAGIC OF ABRAMELIN THE MAGE, translated by S. MacGregor Mathers. Medieval manuscript of ceremonial magic. Basic document in Aleister Crowley, Golden Dawn groups. 268pp. 5⅜ x 8½. 0-486-23211-5

THE BATTLES THAT CHANGED HISTORY, Fletcher Pratt. Eminent historian profiles 16 crucial conflicts, ancient to modern, that changed the course of civilization. 352pp. 5⅜ x 8½. 0-486-41129-X

NEW RUSSIAN-ENGLISH AND ENGLISH-RUSSIAN DICTIONARY, M. A. O'Brien. This is a remarkably handy Russian dictionary, containing a surprising amount of information, including over 70,000 entries. 366pp. 4½ x 6⅛. 0-486-20208-9

NEW YORK IN THE FORTIES, Andreas Feininger. 162 brilliant photographs by the well-known photographer, formerly with *Life* magazine. Commuters, shoppers, Times Square at night, much else from city at its peak. Captions by John von Hartz. 181pp. 9¼ x 10¾. 0-486-23585-8

INDIAN SIGN LANGUAGE, William Tomkins. Over 525 signs developed by Sioux and other tribes. Written instructions and diagrams. Also 290 pictographs. 111pp. 6⅛ x 9¼. 0-486-22029-X

ANATOMY: A Complete Guide for Artists, Joseph Sheppard. A master of figure drawing shows artists how to render human anatomy convincingly. Over 460 illustrations. 224pp. 8⅜ x 11¼. 0-486-27279-6

MEDIEVAL CALLIGRAPHY: Its History and Technique, Marc Drogin. Spirited history, comprehensive instruction manual covers 13 styles (ca. 4th century through 15th). Excellent photographs; directions for duplicating medieval techniques with modern tools. 224pp. 8⅜ x 11¼. 0-486-26142-5

DRIED FLOWERS: How to Prepare Them, Sarah Whitlock and Martha Rankin. Complete instructions on how to use silica gel, meal and borax, perlite aggregate, sand and borax, glycerine and water to create attractive permanent flower arrangements. 12 illustrations. 32pp. 5⅜ x 8½. 0-486-21802-3

EASY-TO-MAKE BIRD FEEDERS FOR WOODWORKERS, Scott D. Campbell. Detailed, simple-to-use guide for designing, constructing, caring for and using feeders. Text, illustrations for 12 classic and contemporary designs. 96pp. 5⅜ x 8½. 0-486-25847-5

THE COMPLETE BOOK OF BIRDHOUSE CONSTRUCTION FOR WOODWORKERS, Scott D. Campbell. Detailed instructions, illustrations, tables. Also data on bird habitat and instinct patterns. Bibliography. 3 tables. 63 illustrations in 15 figures. 48pp. 5¼ x 8½. 0-486-24407-5

SCOTTISH WONDER TALES FROM MYTH AND LEGEND, Donald A. Mackenzie. 16 lively tales tell of giants rumbling down mountainsides, of a magic wand that turns stone pillars into warriors, of gods and goddesses, evil hags, powerful forces and more. 240pp. 5⅜ x 8½. 0-486-29677-6

THE HISTORY OF UNDERCLOTHES, C. Willett Cunnington and Phyllis Cunnington. Fascinating, well-documented survey covering six centuries of English undergarments, enhanced with over 100 illustrations: 12th-century laced-up bodice, footed long drawers (1795), 19th-century bustles, 19th-century corsets for men, Victorian "bust improvers," much more. 272pp. 5⅝ x 8¼. 0-486-27124-2

ARTS AND CRAFTS FURNITURE: The Complete Brooks Catalog of 1912, Brooks Manufacturing Co. Photos and detailed descriptions of more than 150 now very collectible furniture designs from the Arts and Crafts movement depict davenports, settees, buffets, desks, tables, chairs, bedsteads, dressers and more, all built of solid, quarter-sawed oak. Invaluable for students and enthusiasts of antiques, Americana and the decorative arts. 80pp. 6½ x 9¼. 0-486-27471-3

WILBUR AND ORVILLE: A Biography of the Wright Brothers, Fred Howard. Definitive, crisply written study tells the full story of the brothers' lives and work. A vividly written biography, unparalleled in scope and color, that also captures the spirit of an extraordinary era. 560pp. 6⅛ x 9¼. 0-486-40297-5

THE ARTS OF THE SAILOR: Knotting, Splicing and Ropework, Hervey Garrett Smith. Indispensable shipboard reference covers tools, basic knots and useful hitches; handsewing and canvas work, more. Over 100 illustrations. Delightful reading for sea lovers. 256pp. 5⅜ x 8½. 0-486-26440-8

FRANK LLOYD WRIGHT'S FALLINGWATER: The House and Its History, Second, Revised Edition, Donald Hoffmann. A total revision–both in text and illustrations–of the standard document on Fallingwater, the boldest, most personal architectural statement of Wright's mature years, updated with valuable new material from the recently opened Frank Lloyd Wright Archives. "Fascinating"–*The New York Times*. 116 illustrations. 128pp. 9¼ x 10¾. 0-486-27430-6

PHOTOGRAPHIC SKETCHBOOK OF THE CIVIL WAR, Alexander Gardner. 100 photos taken on field during the Civil War. Famous shots of Manassas Harper's Ferry, Lincoln, Richmond, slave pens, etc. 244pp. 10⅜ x 8¼. 0-486-22731-6

FIVE ACRES AND INDEPENDENCE, Maurice G. Kains. Great back-to-the-land classic explains basics of self-sufficient farming. The one book to get. 95 illustrations. 397pp. 5⅜ x 8½. 0-486-20974-1

A MODERN HERBAL, Margaret Grieve. Much the fullest, most exact, most useful compilation of herbal material. Gigantic alphabetical encyclopedia, from aconite to zedoary, gives botanical information, medical properties, folklore, economic uses, much else. Indispensable to serious reader. 161 illustrations. 888pp. 6½ x 9¼. 2-vol. set. (Available in U.S. only.) Vol. I: 0-486-22798-7 Vol. II: 0-486-22799-5

HIDDEN TREASURE MAZE BOOK, Dave Phillips. Solve 34 challenging mazes accompanied by heroic tales of adventure. Evil dragons, people-eating plants, bloodthirsty giants, many more dangerous adversaries lurk at every twist and turn. 34 mazes, stories, solutions. 48pp. 8¼ x 11. 0-486-24566-7

LETTERS OF W. A. MOZART, Wolfgang A. Mozart. Remarkable letters show bawdy wit, humor, imagination, musical insights, contemporary musical world; includes some letters from Leopold Mozart. 276pp. 5⅜ x 8½. 0-486-22859-2

BASIC PRINCIPLES OF CLASSICAL BALLET, Agrippina Vaganova. Great Russian theoretician, teacher explains methods for teaching classical ballet. 118 illustrations. 175pp. 5⅜ x 8½. 0-486-22036-2

THE JUMPING FROG, Mark Twain. Revenge edition. The original story of The Celebrated Jumping Frog of Calaveras County, a hapless French translation, and Twain's hilarious "retranslation" from the French. 12 illustrations. 66pp. 5⅜ x 8½. 0-486-22686-7

BEST REMEMBERED POEMS, Martin Gardner (ed.). The 126 poems in this superb collection of 19th- and 20th-century British and American verse range from Shelley's "To a Skylark" to the impassioned "Renascence" of Edna St. Vincent Millay and to Edward Lear's whimsical "The Owl and the Pussycat." 224pp. 5⅜ x 8½. 0-486-27165-X

COMPLETE SONNETS, William Shakespeare. Over 150 exquisite poems deal with love, friendship, the tyranny of time, beauty's evanescence, death and other themes in language of remarkable power, precision and beauty. Glossary of archaic terms. 80pp. 5³⁄₁₆ x 8¼. 0-486-26686-9

HISTORIC HOMES OF THE AMERICAN PRESIDENTS, Second, Revised Edition, Irvin Haas. A traveler's guide to American Presidential homes, most open to the public, depicting and describing homes occupied by every American President from George Washington to George Bush. With visiting hours, admission charges, travel routes. 175 photographs. Index. 160pp. 8¼ x 11. 0-486-26751-2

THE WIT AND HUMOR OF OSCAR WILDE, Alvin Redman (ed.). More than 1,000 ripostes, paradoxes, wisecracks: Work is the curse of the drinking classes; I can resist everything except temptation; etc. 258pp. 5⅜ x 8½. 0-486-20602-5

SHAKESPEARE LEXICON AND QUOTATION DICTIONARY, Alexander Schmidt. Full definitions, locations, shades of meaning in every word in plays and poems. More than 50,000 exact quotations. 1,485pp. 6½ x 9¼. 2-vol. set. Vol. 1: 0-486-22726-X Vol. 2: 0-486-22727-8

SELECTED POEMS, Emily Dickinson. Over 100 best-known, best-loved poems by one of America's foremost poets, reprinted from authoritative early editions. No comparable edition at this price. Index of first lines. 64pp. 5³⁄₁₆ x 8¼. 0-486-26466-1

THE INSIDIOUS DR. FU-MANCHU, Sax Rohmer. The first of the popular mystery series introduces a pair of English detectives to their archnemesis, the diabolical Dr. Fu-Manchu. Flavorful atmosphere, fast-paced action, and colorful characters enliven this classic of the genre. 208pp. 5³⁄₁₆ x 8¼. 0-486-29898-1

THE MALLEUS MALEFICARUM OF KRAMER AND SPRENGER, translated by Montague Summers. Full text of most important witchhunter's "bible," used by both Catholics and Protestants. 278pp. 6⅝ x 10.   0-486-22802-9

SPANISH STORIES/CUENTOS ESPAÑOLES: A Dual-Language Book, Angel Flores (ed.). Unique format offers 13 great stories in Spanish by Cervantes, Borges, others. Faithful English translations on facing pages. 352pp. 5⅜ x 8½.

0-486-25399-6

GARDEN CITY, LONG ISLAND, IN EARLY PHOTOGRAPHS, 1869–1919, Mildred H. Smith. Handsome treasury of 118 vintage pictures, accompanied by carefully researched captions, document the Garden City Hotel fire (1899), the Vanderbilt Cup Race (1908), the first airmail flight departing from the Nassau Boulevard Aerodrome (1911), and much more. 96pp. 8⅞ x 11¾.   0-486-40669-5

OLD QUEENS, N.Y., IN EARLY PHOTOGRAPHS, Vincent F. Seyfried and William Asadorian. Over 160 rare photographs of Maspeth, Jamaica, Jackson Heights, and other areas. Vintage views of DeWitt Clinton mansion, 1939 World's Fair and more. Captions. 192pp. 8⅞ x 11.   0-486-26358-4

CAPTURED BY THE INDIANS: 15 Firsthand Accounts, 1750-1870, Frederick Drimmer. Astounding true historical accounts of grisly torture, bloody conflicts, relentless pursuits, miraculous escapes and more, by people who lived to tell the tale. 384pp. 5⅜ x 8½.   0-486-24901-8

THE WORLD'S GREAT SPEECHES (Fourth Enlarged Edition), Lewis Copeland, Lawrence W. Lamm, and Stephen J. McKenna. Nearly 300 speeches provide public speakers with a wealth of updated quotes and inspiration—from Pericles' funeral oration and William Jennings Bryan's "Cross of Gold Speech" to Malcolm X's powerful words on the Black Revolution and Earl of Spenser's tribute to his sister, Diana, Princess of Wales. 944pp. 5⅜ x 8⅜.   0-486-40903-1

THE BOOK OF THE SWORD, Sir Richard F. Burton. Great Victorian scholar/adventurer's eloquent, erudite history of the "queen of weapons"—from prehistory to early Roman Empire. Evolution and development of early swords, variations (sabre, broadsword, cutlass, scimitar, etc.), much more. 336pp. 6⅛ x 9¼.

0-486-25434-8

AUTOBIOGRAPHY: The Story of My Experiments with Truth, Mohandas K. Gandhi. Boyhood, legal studies, purification, the growth of the Satyagraha (nonviolent protest) movement. Critical, inspiring work of the man responsible for the freedom of India. 480pp. 5⅜ x 8½. (Available in U.S. only.)   0-486-24593-4

CELTIC MYTHS AND LEGENDS, T. W. Rolleston. Masterful retelling of Irish and Welsh stories and tales. Cuchulain, King Arthur, Deirdre, the Grail, many more. First paperback edition. 58 full-page illustrations. 512pp. 5⅜ x 8½.   0-486-26507-2

THE PRINCIPLES OF PSYCHOLOGY, William James. Famous long course complete, unabridged. Stream of thought, time perception, memory, experimental methods; great work decades ahead of its time. 94 figures. 1,391pp. 5⅜ x 8½. 2-vol. set.
Vol. I: 0-486-20381-6   Vol. II: 0-486-20382-4

THE WORLD AS WILL AND REPRESENTATION, Arthur Schopenhauer. Definitive English translation of Schopenhauer's life work, correcting more than 1,000 errors, omissions in earlier translations. Translated by E. F. J. Payne. Total of 1,269pp. 5⅜ x 8½. 2-vol. set.   Vol. 1: 0-486-21761-2   Vol. 2: 0-486-21762-0

MAGIC AND MYSTERY IN TIBET, Madame Alexandra David-Neel. Experiences among lamas, magicians, sages, sorcerers, Bonpa wizards. A true psychic discovery. 32 illustrations. 321pp. 5⅜ x 8½. (Available in U.S. only.) 0-486-22682-4

THE EGYPTIAN BOOK OF THE DEAD, E. A. Wallis Budge. Complete reproduction of Ani's papyrus, finest ever found. Full hieroglyphic text, interlinear transliteration, word-for-word translation, smooth translation. 533pp. 6½ x 9¼.
0-486-21866-X

HISTORIC COSTUME IN PICTURES, Braun & Schneider. Over 1,450 costumed figures in clearly detailed engravings–from dawn of civilization to end of 19th century. Captions. Many folk costumes. 256pp. 8⅜ x 11¾. 0-486-23150-X

MATHEMATICS FOR THE NONMATHEMATICIAN, Morris Kline. Detailed, college-level treatment of mathematics in cultural and historical context, with numerous exercises. Recommended Reading Lists. Tables. Numerous figures. 641pp. 5⅜ x 8½.
0-486-24823-2

PROBABILISTIC METHODS IN THE THEORY OF STRUCTURES, Isaac Elishakoff. Well-written introduction covers the elements of the theory of probability from two or more random variables, the reliability of such multivariable structures, the theory of random function, Monte Carlo methods of treating problems incapable of exact solution, and more. Examples. 502pp. 5⅜ x 8½. 0-486-40691-1

THE RIME OF THE ANCIENT MARINER, Gustave Doré, S. T. Coleridge. Doré's finest work; 34 plates capture moods, subtleties of poem. Flawless full-size reproductions printed on facing pages with authoritative text of poem. "Beautiful. Simply beautiful."–*Publisher's Weekly.* 77pp. 9¼ x 12. 0-486-22305-1

SCULPTURE: Principles and Practice, Louis Slobodkin. Step-by-step approach to clay, plaster, metals, stone; classical and modern. 253 drawings, photos. 255pp. 8⅛ x 11.
0-486-22960-2

THE INFLUENCE OF SEA POWER UPON HISTORY, 1660–1783, A. T. Mahan. Influential classic of naval history and tactics still used as text in war colleges. First paperback edition. 4 maps. 24 battle plans. 640pp. 5⅜ x 8½. 0-486-25509-3

THE STORY OF THE TITANIC AS TOLD BY ITS SURVIVORS, Jack Winocour (ed.). What it was really like. Panic, despair, shocking inefficiency, and a little heroism. More thrilling than any fictional account. 26 illustrations. 320pp. 5⅜ x 8½.
0-486-20610-6

ONE TWO THREE . . . INFINITY: Facts and Speculations of Science, George Gamow. Great physicist's fascinating, readable overview of contemporary science: number theory, relativity, fourth dimension, entropy, genes, atomic structure, much more. 128 illustrations. Index. 352pp. 5⅜ x 8½. 0-486-25664-2

DALÍ ON MODERN ART: The Cuckolds of Antiquated Modern Art, Salvador Dalí. Influential painter skewers modern art and its practitioners. Outrageous evaluations of Picasso, Cézanne, Turner, more. 15 renderings of paintings discussed. 44 calligraphic decorations by Dalí. 96pp. 5⅜ x 8½. (Available in U.S. only.) 0-486-29220-7

ANTIQUE PLAYING CARDS: A Pictorial History, Henry René D'Allemagne. Over 900 elaborate, decorative images from rare playing cards (14th–20th centuries): Bacchus, death, dancing dogs, hunting scenes, royal coats of arms, players cheating, much more. 96pp. 9¼ x 12¼. 0-486-29265-7

CATALOG OF DOVER BOOKS

MAKING FURNITURE MASTERPIECES: 30 Projects with Measured Drawings, Franklin H. Gottshall. Step-by-step instructions, illustrations for constructing handsome, useful pieces, among them a Sheraton desk, Chippendale chair, Spanish desk, Queen Anne table and a William and Mary dressing mirror. 224pp. 8¼ x 11¼.
0-486-29338-6

NORTH AMERICAN INDIAN DESIGNS FOR ARTISTS AND CRAFTSPEOPLE, Eva Wilson. Over 360 authentic copyright-free designs adapted from Navajo blankets, Hopi pottery, Sioux buffalo hides, more. Geometrics, symbolic figures, plant and animal motifs, etc. 128pp. 8⅜ x 11. (Not for sale in the United Kingdom.)   0-486-25341-4

THE FOSSIL BOOK: A Record of Prehistoric Life, Patricia V. Rich et al. Profusely illustrated definitive guide covers everything from single-celled organisms and dinosaurs to birds and mammals and the interplay between climate and man. Over 1,500 illustrations. 760pp. 7½ x 10¼.   0-486-29371-8

VICTORIAN ARCHITECTURAL DETAILS: Designs for Over 700 Stairs, Mantels, Doors, Windows, Cornices, Porches, and Other Decorative Elements, A. J. Bicknell & Company. Everything from dormer windows and piazzas to balconies and gable ornaments. Also includes elevations and floor plans for handsome, private residences and commercial structures. 80pp. 9⅜ x 12¼.   0-486-44015-X

WESTERN ISLAMIC ARCHITECTURE: A Concise Introduction, John D. Hoag. Profusely illustrated critical appraisal compares and contrasts Islamic mosques and palaces—from Spain and Egypt to other areas in the Middle East. 139 illustrations. 128pp. 6 x 9.   0-486-43760-4

CHINESE ARCHITECTURE: A Pictorial History, Liang Ssu-ch'eng. More than 240 rare photographs and drawings depict temples, pagodas, tombs, bridges, and imperial palaces comprising much of China's architectural heritage. 152 halftones, 94 diagrams. 232pp. 10¾ x 9⅞.   0-486-43999-2

THE RENAISSANCE: Studies in Art and Poetry, Walter Pater. One of the most talked-about books of the 19th century, *The Renaissance* combines scholarship and philosophy in an innovative work of cultural criticism that examines the achievements of Botticelli, Leonardo, Michelangelo, and other artists. "The holy writ of beauty."–Oscar Wilde. 160pp. 5⅜ x 8½.   0-486-44025-7

A TREATISE ON PAINTING, Leonardo da Vinci. The great Renaissance artist's practical advice on drawing and painting techniques covers anatomy, perspective, composition, light and shadow, and color. A classic of art instruction, it features 48 drawings by Nicholas Poussin and Leon Battista Alberti. 192pp. 5⅜ x 8½.
0-486-44155-5

THE MIND OF LEONARDO DA VINCI, Edward McCurdy. More than just a biography, this classic study by a distinguished historian draws upon Leonardo's extensive writings to offer numerous demonstrations of the Renaissance master's achievements, not only in sculpture and painting, but also in music, engineering, and even experimental aviation. 384pp. 5⅜ x 8½.   0-486-44142-3

WASHINGTON IRVING'S RIP VAN WINKLE, Illustrated by Arthur Rackham. Lovely prints that established artist as a leading illustrator of the time and forever etched into the popular imagination a classic of Catskill lore. 51 full-color plates. 80pp. 8⅜ x 11.   0-486-44242-X

HENSCHE ON PAINTING, John W. Robichaux. Basic painting philosophy and methodology of a great teacher, as expounded in his famous classes and workshops on Cape Cod. 7 illustrations in color on covers. 80pp. 5⅜ x 8½.   0-486-43728-0

CATALOG OF DOVER BOOKS

LIGHT AND SHADE: A Classic Approach to Three-Dimensional Drawing, Mrs. Mary P. Merrifield. Handy reference clearly demonstrates principles of light and shade by revealing effects of common daylight, sunshine, and candle or artificial light on geometrical solids. 13 plates. 64pp. 5⅜ x 8½. 0-486-44143-1

ASTROLOGY AND ASTRONOMY: A Pictorial Archive of Signs and Symbols, Ernst and Johanna Lehner. Treasure trove of stories, lore, and myth, accompanied by more than 300 rare illustrations of planets, the Milky Way, signs of the zodiac, comets, meteors, and other astronomical phenomena. 192pp. 8⅜ x 11. 0-486-43981-X

JEWELRY MAKING: Techniques for Metal, Tim McCreight. Easy-to-follow instructions and carefully executed illustrations describe tools and techniques, use of gems and enamels, wire inlay, casting, and other topics. 72 line illustrations and diagrams. 176pp. 8¼ x 10⅞. 0-486-44043-5

MAKING BIRDHOUSES: Easy and Advanced Projects, Gladstone Califf. Easy-to-follow instructions include diagrams for everything from a one-room house for bluebirds to a forty-two-room structure for purple martins. 56 plates; 4 figures. 80pp. 8¾ x 6⅜. 0-486-44183-0

LITTLE BOOK OF LOG CABINS: How to Build and Furnish Them, William S. Wicks. Handy how-to manual, with instructions and illustrations for building cabins in the Adirondack style, fireplaces, stairways, furniture, beamed ceilings, and more. 102 line drawings. 96pp. 8¾ x 6⅜. 0-486-44259-4

THE SEASONS OF AMERICA PAST, Eric Sloane. From "sugaring time" and strawberry picking to Indian summer and fall harvest, a whole year's activities described in charming prose and enhanced with 79 of the author's own illustrations. 160pp. 8¼ x 11. 0-486-44220-9

THE METROPOLIS OF TOMORROW, Hugh Ferriss. Generous, prophetic vision of the metropolis of the future, as perceived in 1929. Powerful illustrations of towering structures, wide avenues, and rooftop parks–all features in many of today's modern cities. 59 illustrations. 144pp. 8¼ x 11. 0-486-43727-2

THE PATH TO ROME, Hilaire Belloc. This 1902 memoir abounds in lively vignettes from a vanished time, recounting a pilgrimage on foot across the Alps and Apennines in order to "see all Europe which the Christian Faith has saved." 77 of the author's original line drawings complement his sparkling prose. 272pp. 5⅜ x 8½. 0-486-44001-X

THE HISTORY OF RASSELAS: Prince of Abissinia, Samuel Johnson. Distinguished English writer attacks eighteenth-century optimism and man's unrealistic estimates of what life has to offer. 112pp. 5⅜ x 8½. 0-486-44094-X

A VOYAGE TO ARCTURUS, David Lindsay. A brilliant flight of pure fancy, where wild creatures crowd the fantastic landscape and demented torturers dominate victims with their bizarre mental powers. 272pp. 5⅜ x 8½. 0-486-44198-9

Paperbound unless otherwise indicated. Available at your book dealer, online at **www.doverpublications.com**, or by writing to Dept. GI, Dover Publications, Inc., 31 East 2nd Street, Mineola, NY 11501. For current price information or for free catalogs (please indicate field of interest), write to Dover Publications or log on to **www.doverpublications.com** and see every Dover book in print. Dover publishes more than 500 books each year on science, elementary and advanced mathematics, biology, music, art, literary history, social sciences, and other areas.